THE BABYLONIAN EXPEDITION

OF

THE UNIVERSITY OF PENNSYLVANIA

SERIES D: RESEARCHES AND TREATISES

EDITED BY

H. V. HILPRECHT

VOL. V, FASCICULUS 2

BY

HUGO RADAU

ECKLEY BRINTON COXE, JUNIOR, FUND"

PHILADELPHIA

Published by the University of Pennsylvania

1910

The Editor determines the material to constitute a volume and reports to the Committee of Publication on the general merits of the manuscript and autograph plates submitted for publication; but the Editor is not responsible for the views expressed by the writer.

NIN-IB
THE DETERMINER OF FATES

ACCORDING TO THE GREAT SUMERIAN EPIC

LUGAL-E ŬG ME-LÁM-BI NER-GÁL

FROM

The Temple Library of Nippur

BY

HUGO RADAU

With Five Halftone Illustrations.

PHILADELPHIA
Published by the University of Pennsylvania
1910

MacCalla & Co. Inc., Printers
Weeks Photo-Engraving Co., Halftones

TO

THE RIGHT REVEREND

Daniel S. Tuttle, D.D., LL.D.,

BISHOP OF MISSOURI AND PRESIDING BISHOP OF THE PROTESTANT EPISCOPAL CHURCH IN THE UNITED STATES OF AMERICA

In Gratefulness, Reverence and Affection

PREFACE.

THE discoverer of the Temple Library of Nippur, Professor H. V. Hilprecht, kindly intrusted me with the publication of the several texts relating to the god "*NIN-IB*, the son of *Enlil*," shortly to be issued in the *Babylonian Expedition*, Series A, Volume XXIX, to which I gave the preliminary title "*Hymns and Prayers to NIN-IB.*"

After a detailed examination of these texts, I found, however, that several of them were neither hymns nor prayers properly speaking, but parts of *epics*. These epics, relating to NIN-IB—the autograph plates of which are to appear in *B. E.*, XXIX—were made the theme of the following pages.

It is, of course, extremely gratifying that the famous Temple Library of Nippur should yield, at the very beginning of its publication, such interesting and important texts as epics, more particularly such epics as were known to us, for the last two decades, from the celebrated Library of Ashshurbânapal. Truly, our most sanguine expectations have been surpassed.

While up to the present time the *terminus a quo* of the Babylonian epical literature was considered to be, at the very earliest, the time of the first dynasty of Babylon, the Temple Library of Nippur pushes this starting point about 500 years ahead, nay, furnishes abundant indirect proofs that the beginning of the Sumerian epical literature antedates even the time of the second dynasty of Ur, or about 2700 B.C.

Not only, however, do the contents of the Temple Library of Nippur push the beginning of the Sumerian epical literature to an almost incredible age, but they help us materially in restoring and correcting the text of the later Assyrian and Neo-Babylonian copies, which, as is only natural, have suffered during the intervening 2000 years some errors and corruptions, thus enabling us to wrest at last the hidden secrets from their hitherto distorted, obscure and difficult passages.

In the following pages I have made an attempt at interpreting the meaning and significance of the epic, "*The royal lord, the fearfulness of whose storm is awe-inspiring.*"

It is well known and admitted by all experts that with regard to its translation this epic is the most difficult of the whole Sumerian and Semitic Babylonian literature. Conscious of this fact, I am far from believing that the translation submitted below is final. I hope, however, that my interpretation will have brought us a good deal nearer to the final goal. Whether I have succeeded in this, time only can tell.

Whenever and wherever several translations of one particular passage might be possible, I have given, in most cases, only one—and this not because I was not conscious of the fact that the one or the other passage might be capable of a different interpretation, but simply because I believe that the *sensus litteralis* or "intended meaning" of each and every human document can be one only. The translations offered below will, therefore, appear to be sometimes quite *subjective*—and subjective they are and will be till I am convinced that the "other possible translation" represents the intended meaning of the original writer or composer.

This subjectivity I extended sometimes even as far as to ignore the later Semitic translations. The Semitic translators exhibit, as do our Sumerian scholars of to-day, various degrees of scholarship: some knew more than others; the translations of some are more accurate and grammatical than those of others; some had before them a better preserved text than others, etc., etc. Whenever, therefore, I thought that the Semitic translator had ignored the rules of Sumerian grammar, I discarded his translation and tried to interpret the original according to what I perceived to be grammatical. I have, however, refrained from giving, in every case, my reasons for doing so. Those who have made the study of the Sumerian grammar their special subject will easily discover the why and wherefore, while those to whom Sumerian grammar is still a *terra incognita* will have either to accept the translations given or to "do better."

It only remains to thank here the authorities of the University of Pennsylvania and of the Museum, Provost C. C. Harrison, President Eckley Brinton Coxe, Jr., S. F. Houston, Chairman of the Babylonian Section, for their continued great courtesies and hospitality during my work in the Museum. To Professor H. V. Hilprecht, my teacher, friend, guide and adviser, who daily and continually encouraged me in these studies by words and deeds, who at all times put his rich experience and profound scholarship most abundantly at my disposal, I owe, of course, my most sincere and profound gratefulness. To Mrs. Sallie Crozer Hilprecht, my gracious benefactress, who again enabled me to continue my studies in the Museum, I cannot but express, publicly, my most heartfelt and sincerest admiration and indebtedness. I am particularly happy to proclaim, *urbi et orbi*, my most profound and sincere reverence and affection for, and gratefulness to, my dear old Bishop, the Right Reverend Daniel S. Tuttle, to whose gentle, gracious and loving kindness and guidance I owe more than words can express. May he accept this little gift as a small token of my lasting gratitude.

HUGO RADAU.

PHILADELPHIA, PA., April 26, 1910.

CONTENTS.

PAGE

I. THE EXISTENCE OF THE TEMPLE LIBRARY OF NIPPUR ATTESTED.... 1–14
1. The Testimony of the Library of Ashshurbânapal........ 1–5
2. The Testimony of the Temple Library of Nippur, based upon
(*a*) The Duplicates within the Temple Library.......... 5–7
(*b*) The Duplicates of Later, *i.e.*, Neo-Babylonian Inscriptions...... 7–8
(*c*) The Duplicates of Texts Antedating the Year 2700 B.C....... 8–12
(*d*) The Duplicates of Texts known from the Library of Ashshurbânapal.......... 12–14
II. THE IMPORTANCE OF THE DUPLICATES OF THE NIPPUR TEMPLE LIBRARY FOR THE STUDY OF THE SUMERIAN LANGUAGE....... 15–18
III. THE SUMERIAN EPIC ENTITLED *lugal-e ûg me-lám-bi ner-gál*, OR "THE ROYAL LORD, THE FEARFULNESS OF WHOSE STORM IS AWE-INSPIRING".......... 19–60
1. The Literature:
(*a*) From the Library of Ashshurbânapal.......... 19–21
(*b*) From the Berlin Museums.......... 21–22
(*c*) From the Temple Library of Nippur.......... 22
2. The Scope and Purpose of the Epic.......... 23–29
IV. TRANSLATIONS.......... 30–60
1. The *ná*ŠU-U and *ná*GA-SUR-RA Stone.......... 31–34
2. The *ná*esi or "Dolerite".......... 34–42
3. The *ná*e-li-el Stone.......... 42–48
4. The *ná*ka-gi-na Stone.......... 48–54
5. The *ná*KA-KA-KAB or *algamêšu* Stone.......... 54–60
V. A FRAGMENT OF THE SUMERIAN EPIC *An-dím dím-ma*, OR "THOU WHO LIKE *Anu* ART MADE.".......... 61–72
VI. PHOTOGRAPHIC REPRODUCTIONS.......... 73

INTRODUCTION.

I

THE EXISTENCE OF THE NIPPUR TEMPLE LIBRARY ATTESTED.

1. The testimony of the Library of Ashshurbânapal.

Soon after the discovery, by Layard and Rassam, about 1850, of the rightly famous Library of Ashshurbânapal, it was learned that many of its literary remains were merely *copies* of older texts preserved in the ancient temples of the Assyrian and Babylonian cities. The subscriptions or colophons at the end of the various tablets from this library state explicitly that this or that document is a copy (*gab-ri*) made (written) from (*šaṭir-ma*) and revised (*bá-rim*) according to the original (*kîma labiri-šù*) kept in such and such a city. Curiously enough, on the basis of Professor Bezold's *Catalogue of the Kouyunjik Collection*, describing the remains of this library, we were enabled to gather that at least *eight* of its tablets were "*copies made from the originals to be found in NIPPUR.*" The eight tablets in question are numbered and described in Bezold's *Catalogue* as follows:

1. "K. 1363. *Incantation*. . . . . Lines 6–12 of reverse form a colophon, in which the text is said to be a copy of an original from Nippur (*gab-ri En-lil^{ki}*)." *Catalogue*, Vol. I, p. 276.

2. "K. 7787. Fragment . . . . of a Sumero-Akkadian *religious* text. According to the colophon it appears to be a copy from a tablet in Nippur (*En-lil^{ki}*)." *Catalogue*, Vol. II, p. 874.

3. "K. 8668. Part of a copy of a *religious*[1](?) text. . . . .

[1] Similar texts in the Nippur Temple Library I have seen and handled. Prof. Hilprecht catalogues them under the heading "phrases methodically arranged."

In the colophon it is stated that the original of this text was found in Nippur; see reverse, l. 2:—*gab-ri En-lil*^{ki}." *Catalogue*, Vol. III, p. 949.

4. "K. 10826. Fragment . . . . of a copy of a *religious* text. According to the colophon (*gab-ri En-lil*^{ki}) its original was written at Nippur." *Catalogue*, Vol. III, p. 1117.

5. "Sm. 491. Copy of a text containing *incantations* with an interlinear Assyrian version; it begins: *én É-NU-RU*[1] *al-DU-ne* [ ]. According to the colophon, the original from which this inscription was copied, was at Nippur; cf. reverse, l. 4:—*gab-ri En-lil*^{ki} *kîma labiri-šù* [*šaṭir-ma bá-rim*]." *Catalogue*, Vol. IV, p. 1412.

6. "Sm. 1117. Part of a text containing *incantations* and directions for *ceremonies*." *Catalogue*, Vol. IV, p. 1464. In the colophon of this tablet we find the annotation *gab-ri En-lil*^{ki}, hence this tablet is likewise a copy of an older Nippur text.

7. "80-7-19, 64. Part of an *astrological* text. According to the colophon it was copied from an original at Nippur (*En-lil*^{ki})." *Catalogue*, Vol. IV, p. 1735.

8 "Bu. 88-5-12, 11 *Hemerology* for the various months. According to the colophon it has been copied from an original in Nippur (*En-lil*^{ki}).[2]" *Catalogue*, Vol. IV, p. 1916.

The testimony of the Library of Ashshurbânapal to the exist-

[1] Several of this class of incantations have been found among the tablets of the Nippur Temple Library and catalogued by Prof. Hilprecht. One of them (Ni. 2187), now preserved in Constantinople, was copied and published by Huber in the *Hilprecht Anniversary Volume*, p. 220. For the text, transcription and translation of Sm. 491 see now Langdon, *Babyloniaca*, III, pp. 28, 31.

[2] The text was published by Bezold (*Z. A.*, 1888, pp. 245ff.) and Pinches (*C. T.*, IV, 5, 6), and translated by Boissier in *P. S. B. A.*, XXIV, pp. 220ff. The subscription of this tablet reads: *gab-ri En-lil*^{ki} *kîma labiri-šù šaṭir*(= *ŠAR*) *-ma bá*(= *EŠ*)*-rim*.

ence of a possible library at Nippur is, therefore, quite plain and explicit. On the strength of such statements perhaps it was that the University of Pennsylvania equipped, most generously, its several expeditions to excavate at Nippur and to recover, if possible, the remains of that famous library.[1] Its efforts were crowned with instantaneous success. At the very beginning, during the *first expedition*, the spade of the excavator uncovered part of that library. This was about twenty years ago. But as the mass of the texts constituting the Nippur Temple Library has to be assigned to the time of the second dynasty of Ur, and the first half of the first dynasty of Isin, or about 2700–2400 B.C., thus antedating that of Ashshurbânapal by about 2000 years,[2] and as the tablets recovered are all written in Old Babylonian characters and for the greater part in the Sumerian language—either *EME-KU* or *EME-SAL*—it was only natural that the true nature of the tablets, thus unearthed, should not have been generally recognized, that the importance of the find should have been even misunderstood, that the value of the gem, thus discovered, should have been underestimated. We all know that twenty years ago our knowledge of the Sumerian language, our ability to read Old Babylonian cuneiform signs, was extremely limited. No wonder, therefore, that the tablets unearthed during the earlier expeditions were treated by some members of this scientific undertaking as being of comparatively little importance and value. Such an impression, being based upon an imperfect and inadequate *knowledge* of the Sumerian language *of twenty years ago*, cannot, however, be made to be *standard* or *norm according to which the collection* of Babylonian tablets, preserved in the Museum of the University of Pennsylvania, *is to be judged*

[1] Cf. Peters, *Nippur*, Vol. II, p. 109.

[2] See *Hilprecht Anniversary Volume*, pp. 388ff., and Hilprecht, *B. E.*, Series D, Vol. I, Fasciculus 1, p. 7.

at this present time. Science, happily, is progressive, and this is particularly the case with the science of Assyriology and Sumeriology, where the results of to-day may be, and very often are, flatly contradicted by those of to-morrow.

True it is, that even now our knowledge of Sumerian is very limited, that, owing to the absence of a grammar and a dictionary of this language, we are very often obliged to grope in the dark; but likewise it must be admitted that especially during the last ten years the study of the Sumerian has made such tremendous strides forward that very soon it will rank with Assyriology and the other Semitic languages as an exact science. Scholars who have kept pace with the progress of Sumeriology will, I am sure, readily agree with me on this point; those to whom Sumeriology is still a *tabula rasa*, a *tohû-wa-bohû*, will either have to admit that they are no longer leaders but merely followers, or will have to make a desperate effort to "keep up."

And because he did "keep up" with the progress of Sumeriology to such an extent as to be easily the leader of all American Sumeriologists, therefore Prof. Hilprecht was in a position, more than a decade ago, to recognize the true value of the gem unearthed at Nippur, and proclaimed, publicly, the discovery of the Nippur Temple Library—a discovery so tremendous in its extent and consequences, so revolutionizing[1] in our conception of history, religion and culture that one cannot as yet grasp its full meaning and significance.

Having occupied myself, during the last two years, almost exclusively with the examination and the study of the literary remains of the Nippur Temple Library, I do not hesitate to state, without fear of contradiction, that the discovery of the Nippur Temple Library by Prof. H. V. Hilprecht marks the beginning

[1] Cf. Pinches' very appropriate remarks in the *London Times* of March 30, 1910, p. 4.

of a new epoch in the study of Sumerian. *What the Library of Ashshurbânapal has been and still is for the study of the Assyrian, the Library of Nippur will be for the study of the Sumerian language.*

As in every case, when one makes a great discovery, so in this case, scholars necessarily at first were somewhat sceptical, and this, no doubt, from an unprejudiced and purely scientific standpoint. A discovery like the one made by Prof. Hilprecht is too great, and in its consequences too far-reaching, to be accepted without any further proof than the mere "say-so" of the discoverer. To a certain degree, therefore, everyone is justified in his attitude of scepticism, till absolute and indisputable proofs are forthcoming that the contents of the Nippur Temple Library are as important as represented and in all respects the same as or similar to those of Ashshurbânapal's Library.

2. The Testimony of the Temple Library of Nippur, Based upon its Duplicates.

It would seem a little premature to make, at this time, a comparison between the two libraries, seeing that so far only thirty plates of inscriptions of a more or less literary character have been published[1] in addition to the *Mathematical, Metrological and Chronological Tablets*, issued by Prof. Hilprecht in *B. E.*, XX[1]. But though anticipating future publications, yet a comparison of this kind would, I think, be most helpful and instructive even now.

Again and again it has been pointed out that the many *duplicates* in the Library of Ashshurbânapal prove beyond a reasonable shadow of a doubt its true and real character. These duplicates are of a threefold character, viz., (*a*) those of tablets within

[1] By the writer in the *Hilprecht Anniversary Volume*. Others will appear soon in my forthcoming volume on *Hymns and Prayers to NIN-IB, B. E.*, XXIX, Part 1.

the library; (*b*) those of the later or Neo-Babylonian period, and lastly, (*c*) those of the earlier or Old Babylonian inscriptions.

Can we, at this time, point to similar characteristics? Can we show that there appear in the Nippur Temple Library the same or similar phenomena? Can we, to put it briefly, point out duplicates which prove for the Nippur Temple Library what those of Ashshurbânapal's Library are said to demonstrate for the latter?

(*a*) *Duplicates within the Temple Library.*

1. The "hymn in praise of the mightiness of *Nin-an-sí-an-na*," published in the *Hilprecht Anniversary Volume*, No. 2,[1] is a duplicate of the last part of *C. B. M.* 11,391,[2] Rev., col. IV, 21ff.

2. *B. E.*, XXIX, No. 2,[3] a "hymn praising NIN-IB as Babylonia's 'saviour' from the oppressive yoke and bondage of the enemy" is a duplicate of *B. E.*, XXIX, No. 3.[3]

3. *B. E.*, XXIX, No. 7 : 1–13[4] is a duplicate of both *B. E.*, XXIX, No. 6, Rev., col. II, 18f.[5], and of *B. E.*, XXIX, No. 8,[6]

[1] For photographic reproduction see *l. c.*, pls. II, III, and for transcription and translation, *l.c.*, pp. 391ff.

[2] So far unpublished, but see the photographic reproduction in the *Hilprecht Anniversary Volume*, pl. IV. For further details cf. *ibidem*, p. 401, note 14; p. 446, 2; p. 453, 7, and pl. 1, No. 2, *Additions and Variations*.

[3] For autograph text, transcription and translation of these two tablets see my forthcoming volume on *Sumerian Hymns and Prayers to NIN-IB*. For the present cf. below, pp. 24ff.

[4] Cf. photographic reproduction, pl. III.

[5] This line ought to be restored: [*lugal-mu* (or *ur-sag-e*) *náSA*]*G-KAL-e ba-gub*. For photographic reproduction see pl. I. The reason why I prefer to restore as given rather than [*lugal-mu ná*]*esi-e ba-gub* is this: In *A. S. K. T.*, p. 81 : 23, cf. *Ninrag*, p. 42 : 23, the following stones are mentioned: *náSU-U*, *náSAG-KAL*, *náesi*, *náUZ*, *náka-gi-na* and *nágiš-šir-gal* (l. 25), of which *náSAG-KAL*, *náesi*, *náka-gi-na* occur also in *B. E.*, XXIX, No. 7, which is, as we shall see, the "11th tablet of *lugal-e ŭg me-lám-bi ner-gál*." The 12th tablet begins with the *nágiš-šir-gal* (Abel-Winckler, *Keilschrifttexte*, p. 60). The [*náSA*]*G-KAL*

col. II, 1-4,[7] all three recording the fate of the *ná*SAG-KAL stone determined by NIN-IB.

4. *B. E.*, XXIX, No. 7: 14-29[8] is a duplicate of *B. E.*, XXIX, No. 8, col. II, 5-14[9] in both NIN-IB determines the fate of the "dolerite," *i.e.*, the *ná*esi = *abnu*ušû.

5. *B. E.*, XXIX, No. 7: 52-59, being part of the fate of the *ná*ka-gi-na stone, is a duplicate of No. 6, Rev., col. III, 1-8.[10]

(b) Duplicates of the Later, i.e., Neo-Babylonian Period.

6. The "prayer of *Nin-Mar*" published in the *Hilprecht Anniversary Volume*, No. 3 : 1-11,[11] is apparently the original of *R. H.*, p. 101 : 8, 9—102 : 28, 29 (here with a Semitic translation).

7. *B. E.*, XXIX, No. 8, col. III, 1-6 (NIN-IB curses the *Algamêshu* = *ná*KAK-KAB) and *l.c.*, ll. 7ff. (the fate of the *ná*dŭ-ši-a

of *B. E.*, XXIX, No. 6, Rev., col. II, 18, is preceded by the *ná*ŠU-U, and in *A. S. K. T.*, p. 81 : 23, by *ná*SU-U, hence *ná*SU-U = *ná*ŠU-U; for the interchange of *s* and *š* see *Hilprecht Anniversary Volume*, p. 405, note 36, and Fossey, *ibidem*, p. 119, No. 43. From this it follows (*a*) that *B. E.*, XXIX, No. 8, col. II, follows, after a break of about six lines, upon *B. E.*, XXIX, No. 6, Rev., col. II—the width of both columns agrees exactly, it being 4, 5 cm.—hence *B. E.*, XXIX, No. 7 : 1-3 = No. 6, Rev., col. II, 18-20; *B. E.*, XXIX, No. 7 : 4-9 = broken away; *B. E.*, XXIX, No. 7 : 10-13 = No. 8, col. II, 1-4; (*b*) that the *ná*SU-U or *ná*ŠU-U formed, in all probability, the end of the "10th tablet of *lugal-e ŭg me-lám-bi ner-gál*;" (*c*) that No. 6, Rev., col. III, 1-8, forms the duplicate of No. 7 : 52-59, *i.e.*, it belongs to the *ná*ka-gi-na mentioned in the 11th tablet of the same epic.

[6] Cf. photographic reproduction, pl. II.

[7] More accurately ll. 1-4 correspond to No. 7 : 10-13.

[8] Cf. photographic reproduction, pl. III.

[9] More particularly ll. 5-14 is = No. 7 : 14-23. For photographic reproduction see pl. II.

[10] See above, p. 6, note 5, *c*.

[11] For photographic reproduction see *ibidem*, pl. V, and for transcription and translation, *l.c.*, pp. 436ff.

stone) is the original of *V. A. Th.* 251[1] : 18ff., and 30ff.—the 12th tablet of the epic *lugal-e ŭg me-lám-bi ner-gál*, which was written (*IN-ŠÁR-ma*) by a certain *m d EN-iqîša*[sha], the son of *m d AG-še-e-mi*, who deposited (*DU-in*) it "for the prolongation of his life (*ana TIN-ZI* mesh-*šu*) in *É-zi-da*, the house of his lordship."[2]

8. *B. E.*, XXIX, Nos. 2 and 3[3] are duplicates of *R. H.*, p. 123 (No. 71), here with a Semitic translation. Line 3 of the Neo-Babylonian copy corresponds to l. 12 of Nos. 2 and 3. With the help of the corresponding tablets from the Nippur Temple Library I was enabled to restore both the Sumerian text and its Semitic translation. Seeing that this text is one of the most important ones of all inscriptions so far published, I have given a transcription and translation of it in my forthcoming volume, *B. E.*, XXIX.

(c) Duplicates of Texts Antedating the Second Dynasty of Ur or c. 2700 B. C.

Though I can not, at this time, point to a single instance or a particular specimen which would show that the tablets of the "Older Temple Library of Nippur" contained copies of still older texts, yet indirect proof is abundantly at hand which would raise the presumption in favor of this contention to almost a

[1] Published by Abel-Winckler, *Keilschrifttexte*, p. 60 : 18—p. 61 : 29, and p. 61, 30ff.; cf. Hommel, *Sumerische Lesestücke*, p. 123 : 18ff.

[2] *Ina É-zi-da bît be-lu-ti-šù*. Notice here that a tablet apparently praising the god NIN-IB as the determiner of the fates of the several stones is deposited in *É-zi-da*, the temple of the god *Nabû*! From this it follows that *EN-iqîša* regarded NIN-IB, the "Son" of the Nippur trinity and god of *É-šu-me-du*, to be the same as *Nabû*, the "Son" of the Babylon trinity and god of *É-zi-da*—both were, as "sons," the gods who could prolong life! For *d*NIN-IB = *d AG*, see *C. T.*, XXV, 11 : 12 = 15, III, 2; for *d*NIN-IB as "god of life," cf. *Hilprecht Anniversary Volume*, pp. 423–425, and for *d AG* as the *mu-bal-liṭ mi-i-ti* see IV. *R*²., 53 *c*, col. IV, 33, 35. The "Son" of every Babylonian trinity is the "great physician and healer, the life-giver and deliverer from death, destruction and hades."

[3] See already above, p. 6, 2.

certainty. I am very well conscious of the unique importance and far-reaching consequences of this assertion, for if this can be proved or, at least, made probable, it would put the height of the Sumerian period in the Babylonian civilization so far ahead, in point of time, of that of all other nations as to be without parallel in the history of mankind. Indications, pointing in this direction, are undoubtedly at hand, and I beg to submit some of them here, reserving a full discussion of this problem for the future, until more of the tablets of the Temple Library of Nippur have been published and translated.

(α) In the *Hilprecht Anniversary Volume*, p. 436, I drew the attention of the student to a remarkable passage in one of the hymns there published, saying "on the reverse of No. 3 the goddess *Nin-Mar* addresses the god NIN-IB, telling him of her grief and entreating him to use his influence with his father to comply with her wishes. To make this entreaty more effective, NIN-IB is asked to lift up his eyes to *Enlil* in prayer and to recite before him *the old hymn 'My city is destroyed, in weeping I cry!'*" This passage proves clearly that as early as 2700–2400 B.C. certain older and well-known hymns were inserted into others, as circumstances might or might not demand. Exactly the same phenomena may be observed in our Bible, where likewise certain *older* hymns as, *e.g.*, "the song of Lamech" (Gen., 4 : 23, 24), or "the song of Deborah" (Judges, 5 : 2-31) were inserted by the later writers of the several books.

(β) If we compare the text of *B. E.*, XXIX, No. 2, with that of No. 3, we will have to admit that, though the inscriptions are apparently identical, their several *variants*[1] point unmistakably

[1] Cf., *e.g.*, *a-ri dŭ-dŭ-dŭ* = *a-ri-ri dŭ-šù-dŭ-dŭ*; *ù-ŭg-zal-li-da-dím* = *zal-li-da-dím*; *ri-a* = *é-ri-a*, l. 2.—*dusu* = ^{gish}*dusu*, l. 4.—*kalam* = *gú-kalam*, l. 6.—*ì-ne-šú* = *ì-ne-a*, l. 21.—*sú(g)-zag-gâ-a* = *zaḫ-ga*, l. 23.—*dù-da(l)* = *dù-dé*, l. 30.—*íb-[ni-]da* = *íb-ba-na*, l. 39, etc. For still other variants see the transcription in *B. E.*, XXIX.

to a much older and common source from which these two editions flowed, but if this be admitted, then No. 2 and No. 3 must be independent copies of an older text. The same observation holds true when we compare *B. E.*, XXIX, No. 7 with *l. c.*, No. 8, col. II. Though both inscriptions are, no doubt, "duplicates," yet the *variants*[1] can not be accounted for except on the supposition that each text had its own literary history, pointing to a time far beyond that of 2700 B.C.

(γ) Even the celebrated *hymn*[2] *chanted by king Idîn-Dagan* in the temple of Nippur on New Year's day cannot have been composed during the time of the kings of Isin. Against such a supposition speak (1) the *variants*[3] of *H. A. V.*, No. 2, compared with *C. B. M.* 11,391; (2) the *religious background*, which, as has been pointed out (*l. c.*, pp. 407ff.), portrays the time of about 5700 B.C. Hence this hymn was merely *adapted* to the time of the I. dynasty of Isin, was *made to suit* the new conditions prevalent at about 2400 B.C.

(δ) The *commands pronounced by NIN-IB* with regard to the fate of the "*dolerite*," *B. E.*, XXIX, No. 7 : 26–29,

"If a king for the prolongation of his life
his name, lo, inscribes,
"If his statue for future days,
lo, he builds;
"Into the *É-minnû*, (the place) of wonders,
the temple full of delights,

[1] Cf. *náesi-a* = *náesi-e*; *im-ma-gub* = *ba-gub*, l. 14(5).—*nam-ám-mi-[ib-tar-ri]* = *nam-im-mi-ib-tar-ri*, l. 16(7).— *i-izi-dím* = *i-izi-dugud-dím*, l. 18(9).—*dEn-lil-lá-ra* = *dEn-lil-lá-ge*, l. 21(12).—For other variants see the transcription given below, pp. 34ff.

[2] Published and translated by me in the *Hilprecht Anniversary Volume*, pp. 391ff.

[3] See *H. A. V.*, No. 2, pl. 1, *Additions and Variations*.

"To the place where one (*i.e.*, the gods) drink(s) water,
lo, he shall bring thee,
for an ornament he shall erect thee,"

have been strictly adhered to by Gudea, patesi of Lagash, who reports, Statue B, col. VII, that he caused to be brought, from the mountain of Magan, a dolerite out of which he made a statue (ll. 10-13), putting it up in *É-ninnû* (ll. 19, 20) at the *ki-a-nag*, *i.e.*, "the place where (the gods) drink water (l. 55)." But from this it follows that *B. E.*, XXIX, No. 7, must have been known to Gudea who admittedly lived *before* the time of the kings of the II. dynasty of Ur.[1]

(ε) Lastly, the unpoetical "*editorial annotation*" found, *e.g.*, in *B. E.*, XXIX, No. 7 : 60-61,

"Now (this) was among the fates (determined) by NIN-IB
at the time when the *ka-gi-na* stone was found (lived)
in the country. (And) thus, lo, it was!"

reminds us evidently of our "once upon a time," *i.e.*, it intends to describe something which happened in *times long passed by;* but by doing this it is, *ipso facto*, an indisputable witness or testimony to the old, very old age of this class of texts.

These are some of the considerations which, when their significance and meaning are duly appreciated, must irresistibly lead one to the conclusion that the Temple Library of Nippur, though confessedly the oldest in the world, to a great extent contains texts which must have been in existence long before the second dynasty of Ur or about 2700 B.C., thus being a mute, but never-

[1] I arrive, therefore, at a conclusion opposite to that of Hrozný, *Ninrag*, p. 64: "*Daraus folgt selbstverständlich, dass unser Epos nicht vor Gudea entstanden sein kann, was übrigens auch aus anderen Gründen unwahrscheinlich wäre.*" Will Hrozný oblige me by giving his "other reasons"?

theless most emphatic, witness to the great age of the Sumerian civilization and religion.

(*d*) *Duplicates of Texts known from the Library of Ashshurbânapal.*

Repeatedly the question has been asked, whether there exist in the Temple Library of Nippur duplicate tablets of those known from the Library of Ashshurbânapal. That such duplicates would be found some day, was certain; it only was necessary to wait till those who at the present are engaged in the publication of the Nippur Temple Library would be lucky enough to discover or recognize them. Both Prof. Hilprecht and I are in the fortunate position to announce to the learned world that several of such texts have been found, all of which will be published and pointed out at the proper time and place. For the present I may be permitted to draw the attention of scholars to the following texts which will appear in autograph reproduction in my forthcoming volume on "Hymns and Prayers to *NIN-IB*."

9. *B. E.*, XXIX, No. 9, Obv., ll. 1ff. (cf. photographic reproduction, pl. V, Nos. 6, 7), is represented in Ashshurbânapal's Library by K. 2864, 15ff. (here with a Semitic translation), published by Hrozný, *Ninrag, Taf.* I, and transcribed and translated, *l. c.*, p. 6. According to the colophon of the K. tablet, this inscription is part of the *dub I kam-ma An-dím dím-ma, i.e.*, "the first tablet of 'Thou who like Anu art made,'" being followed by the "second tablet," which began with the words [gish]*ginar za-gín-na ní-ḫuš* [*ba-ū*], *i.e.*, "Upon a bright wagon the one of terrible fearfulness [rode]."

10. *B. E.*, XXIX, No. 9, Rev., ll. 2ff., is known to us from two copies of the Library of Ashshurbânapal, viz., from Rm. 117, Rev., ll. 1ff., and its duplicate, K. 4829, Rev. (both with a Semitic translation). Line 1 of the latter tablet corresponds to our No. 9 : 5. These inscriptions were likewise published by Hrozný,

Ninrag, *Taf*. X (Rm. 117, Rev.) and *Taf*. VIII (K. 2829, Rev.) and translated *ibidem*, p. 18. According to the colophon, preserved on K. 2829, which reads *dub III* [+ x]-*kam-ma An-dím dím-ma zag-til-la-bi-šú*, this inscription formed "the three + xth tablet of 'Thou who like Anu art made.' End." From this it follows that *B. E.*, XXIX, No. 9, is a fragment of a larger inscription containing the 1-6th (thus I would emend the III + x of K. 2829) tablet of the epic *An-dím dím-ma*.

11. *B. E.*, XXIX, No. 7 (cf. photographic reproduction, pls. III, IV, Nos. 4, 5) in all respects—excepting, of course, the *later* variants—is a duplicate of the following numbers from the Library of Ashshurbânapal, viz., K. 2862 + K. 2868 + K. 5065 + 81-7-27, 120 + additions as given in IV. *R*²., p. 2 *b*. All of these numbers have been edited in IV. *R*²., 13, No. 1, and are translated by Hrozný, *Ninrag*, pp. 22ff.

Though the Nippur tablet has, as is generally the case, no subscription whatever, yet from the colophon of the later copies from Ashshurbânapal's Library we learn that it is the

dub XI kam-ma lugal-e ŭg me-lám-bi ner-gál
kîma labiri-šù šaṭir(=*ŠÁR*)-*ma* [*bá-rim*], *i.e.*,

"The 11th tablet of '*The royal lord, the fearfulness of whose storm is awe-inspiring* (*mighty*).'
"Like its original copied and compared."

B. E., XXIX, No. 7, is thus proved to belong to the great *epic* which began with the words, "The royal lord, etc."

Above[1] I have pointed out that *B. E.*, XXIX, No. 8, col. II, continues, *l. c.*, No. 6, Rev., col. II, and that No. 8, col. III, 1-6,[2] is the original of *V. A. Th.*, 251,[3] which has the following colophon:

[1] See p. 6, note 5, *a*.
[2] See p. 7, 7.
[3] Abel-Winckler, *Keilschrifttexte*, p. 60.

44-*ám mu šid-bi dub XII kam lugal-e ŭg me-lám-bi ner-gál nu-al-til gab-ri Bár-sib^{ki} ki-ma la-bi-ri-šu, i.e.,*

"44 lines in all (its number). The 12th tablet of 'The royal lord, the fearfulness of whose storm is awe-inspiring.'

"Incomplete. Duplicate of (a) Borsippa (tablet); like its original (*sc.* copied and compared)."

Hence *B. E.*, XXIX, Nos. 6 + 8 belong (together with No. 7) to the same series; contain, in fact, parts of the VI., VII.,[1] X.,[2] XI.,[3] XII.[4] and XIII.[5] tablet of this famous epic.

The net result of this short investigation may briefly be summed up as follows:

The Temple Library of Nippur, like that of Ashshurbânapal, does contain duplicates of various literary productions: out of *the several inscriptions so far published, eleven*—or more than the fourth part—*are duplicates of one kind or another*; *it counts among its treasures epics, and these in several redactions* (Nos. 6 + 8 is a different redaction from that of No. 7), *one of which was, no doubt, the original from which the copy of Ashshurbânapal's Library was made*, either directly or indirectly. Surely a most favorable and auspicious sign for the possibilities of the Temple Library of Nippur.

[1] No. 6, Obv., cols. I, II. Or do these lines belong to tablets V, VII or VI, VIII?

[2] No. 6, Rev., cols. I–II, 17; No. 8, Rev., col. I.

[3] No. 6, Rev., col. II, 18ff.; No. 8, Rev., col. II; No. 6, Rev., col. III = No. 7 : 1ff.

[4] No. 8, Rev., col. III.

[5] No. 8, Rev., col. IV.

II.

THE IMPORTANCE OF THE DUPLICATES OF THE NIPPUR TEMPLE LIBRARY FOR THE STUDY OF THE SUMERIAN LANGUAGE.

DUPLICATES like those enumerated above are of inestimable value not only for the historical study of the Sumerian language and literature, but also and especially for its grammar and lexicon. With their help we can trace the history of a text during 2000 years of Babylonian literary activity; can point out, how glosses,[1] words[2] or even whole lines[3] have crept into it; can uncover its corruptions;[4] can enrich the lexicon by means of the various phonetic writings[5] and variants;[6] can establish new grammatical rules, as, *e.g.*, the difference between the pronominal suffixes *-mu*, *-zu*,

[1] See *Hilprecht Anniversary Volume*, p. 440, notes 1–3.

[2] *L. c.*, p. 437 : 5, *(azag) ga-ša-an*; *i-izi-(dugud-) dím*, *B. E.*, XXIX, No. 7: 18(9), see below, p. 36, etc.

[3] *Ninrag*, p. 31 : 26, 27, see below, p. 58, and *l.c.*, p. 27 : 11, 12, see below, p. 44, are not found in the Nippur texts.

[4] *dMu-ul-lil-lá* for better *dMu-ul-lil-li*, *Hilprecht Anniversary Volume*, p. 440, note 1; *ḫar-sag* corrupted from *ša(g)-ḫar-sag-ga-ka*, *B. E.*, XXIX, No. 7 : 15; *náa-lá-lum* for *náa-lá-lum-ma*, *l.c.*, No. 7 : 38, etc. Cf. also below, p. 17, note 2.

[5] Cf., *e.g.*, *galuna(d)* = *galune*, *B. E.*, XXIX, No. 7 : 40; *ge* = *me-en* = *gi*, for *gin* or *mèn*, *l.c.*, 7 : 58; *náe-li-el* = *náa-lá-lum*, *l.c.*, 7 : 38; *náŠU-U* = *náSU-U*, above, p. 6, note 5; *si-gi* = *sí(g)*, 7 : 54; *šár* = *sar*, *B. E.*, XXIX, No. 2 : 8; *gu-ru-um* = *gu-ru-un*, l. 15; *á-bí* = *ní-bi*, l. 16; *ūr-ūr* = *ur-ur*, l. 24; *gú-gur-gur* (or *gà-gà*?) = *gú-gar-gar* = *gurum-ag* = *gurun-gar*, see note 13 to *B.E.*, XXIX, Nos. 2, 3 : 15, etc.

[6] See, *e.g.*, above, p. 9, note 1; p. 10, note 1.

-ni, *-bi* on the one hand and *-mà*,[1] *-za*,[2] *-na*,[3] *-ba*[4] on the other—a difference which, it seems, has escaped the attention of the Sumeriologists.[5] So far I have not yet found one single example in the

[1] The pronominal suffixes in *a* stand *always* and *invariably* for *-mu*, *-zu*, *-ni*, *-bi* + a postposition, hence *mà* = *mu-a* (*šú*, *ta*, *ra*, *da*, etc.) can never express a *nominative* or *accusative*. Cyl. A, 10 : 24–26, *É-bàr-bàr ki á-ág-gà-mà ki* ^d^*Babbar-dím dalla-a-mà ki-ba*, etc., can be translated only by "in my *É-bàr-bàr*, the place of the oracles, in my place which shines like the sun, in that place," etc.; Cyl. A, 5 : 12, *sib-mu ma-mu-zu mà ga-mu-ra-búr-búr* is rather "my shepherd, thy dream *concerning* (*about*) *me* I will explain unto thee;" Cyl. A, 9 : 10, *garza-mà*, "the commands of mine" (*i.e.*, issued by me); *l.c.*, l. 20, *mà* ^d^*Nin-Gir-su*, "for me, N.;" *l.c.*, l. 23, "(my temple is the *É-ninnû*) *mà en-kur-ra ab-si(g)-a*, which (*a*) for me, the lord of the world, lo, has been made to abound in splendor."

[2] Cf. *dingir-za ḫe-ḫul*, "in thy god rejoice," *H. A. V.*, 19 : 21; *i-dé-za*, "the eyes of thine," *l.c.*, 3 : 23; *é-za*, "(un)to thy house," *l.c.*, 19 : 16.

[3] See Cyl. A, 5 : 18, *éš É-ninnû-na dū-ba za-ra ma-ra-an-dú(g)*, "he gave command to thee (with regard) to (the) build(ing) *at* his house, the *E.*," thus showing that Gudea was not its original builder, but merely one who built *at* it; similarly Cyl. A, 16 : 8; 20 : 9; 24 : 8. *Lit-e edin-na-na er-gí(g) mu-un-ma-al* = *lit-tim ANA bîti-ŠU mar-ṣi-iš i-bak-ki*, *R. H.*, 101 : 51, 52 = 116c : 3, 4.

[4] Cyl. A, 1 : 25, *dú(g)-ba ḫa-mu-da-túm*, "by means of (with, in: *ba* = *bi-da*) these words I will express it;" Cyl. A, 6 : 5, ("the second one is the god *Nin-dub*) *é-a giš-ḫar-ba im-mi-sí(g)-sí(g)-gi*, who (*gi*), lo, has traced the temple in (!) its outlines;" IV. *R.*,[2] 27, No. 1 : 8–11, ^gish^*a-am šita(n)-na-ba*(!) *nu-su(g)-ga-mu*, ^gish^*a-am ùr-ra-ba*(!) *ab-sir-ra-mu*, "a willow which (*ga*) by (*ba*) its irrigation-canal (*INA ra-ṭi-ŠU*) is not watered, I (am); a willow which (*ra*) by (*ba*) its very roots (*iš-da-nu-uš* = *INA išdâni-ŠU*) is plucked out, I (am)," thus complains Ishtar while drawing near to the abode of the *ú-sag-gà*.

[5] Though *Langdon*, generally a keen observer of the translations of Thureau-Dangin, in *Babyloniaca*, vol. I, p. 215 *et passim*, makes the partly correct statement that *ba*, *ma*, etc., express the *status obliquus*, yet on the very same page he follows Thureau-Dangin so closely as to ignore his own rule. Cf. *l.c.*, p. 215, a passage from Cyl. A, VI, 1, 2, *mul-azag-ba* = "*l'étoile pure*," instead of "(all that which concerns the building of the temple she will announce unto thee) by a bright star;" *l.c.*, p. 214, a passage from Cyl. A, IX, 8, *pa-te-si é-mu ma-dū-na* = "*le patési qui construira mon temple pour moi*," instead of "unto the patesi who, etc." Examples like these are numerous, showing that even Langdon did ignore or not recognize this rule in most, if not all, those cases where his predecessors have ignored it.

Old Babylonian inscriptions which would indicate that this "fine distinction" has been ignored.[1] With the help of the Nippur texts I was, however, able to discover, in the later Assyrian and Neo-Babylonian copies, several infractions[2] into this rule, showing

[1] In this connection it ought to be observed that the so-called "*status constructus*" does not exist in Sumerian. The *two nouns* (!) thus connected are considered to be a *composite noun*, cf. the German "*das Land meines Vaters*" = "*mein Vaterland*," hence the *nomen rectum*, though in the *status obliquus* has *mu* : *é-a-a-mu* (not *mà*) = "*mein Vaterhaus*." But if such a *composite noun* with pronominal suffix is dependent upon a postposition or other noun, the pronominal suffix must show, of course, the forms in *a*. Cyl. A, 5 : 10, *á-zid-da lugal-mà-ge*, "at (*da*) my (*mà*) king's (*ge*) right (side);" cf. also Cyl. A, 6 : 12, *á-zid-da lugal-zag-ge*. If a noun and *pronominal suffix* stand in a so-called *status constructus* relation then the suffix (because not a noun!) must show the form in *a*: "thy eyes" = *i-dé-zu*; "the eyes of thine" = *i-dé-za*.

[2] To mention a few examples here, I may draw the attention to the following: The correct *ma-a-a-ba* of *Hilprecht Anniversary Volume*, p. 437 : 9 and note 13, is corrupted in the Neo-Babylonian copy to *ma-a-(a-)bi* (*ma-a-a* = "where," *e-ka-a*; *ma-a-a-bi* = "its where;" *ma-a-a-ba* = "to its where, whereto," *e-ki-am*). The correct *mé-ma* of *B. E.*, XXIX, No. 7 : 17 (and parallel passage) is corrupted, in the text from Ashshurbânapal's Library, to *mé-mu* though correctly translated by *INA ta-ḫa-zi-IA*, see below, p. 37 : 8; while the correct *á nam-ur-sag-gà-mu* is wrongly rendered by *a-na i-di qar-ra-du-ti-ia*, *l.c.*, 1, 25. *Erim-mu egir-mu-a* of *C. T.*, XV, 25 : 20 (which originally formed a part of the Nippur Temple Library, see *Hilprecht Anniversary Volume*, p. 385, note 3), shows in the Assyrian duplicate, K. 41, III, 10, the corruption *úru* (for *erim*)-*MÀ egir*-MU, though quite rightly translated by *a-li* (for *maštaki*) *ar-ki-ia* (= *arkî-ia* = *ina ar-ki-ia!*).

This last example is of the highest importance for the *Assyrian grammar*, showing us that the same phenomenon is to be met with even in the Semitic-Babylonian language. The Assyrian pronominal suffix "my," *e.g.*, is only *i*, never *ia*, *va*; but wherever *ia*, *va* occurs, it is a clear indication that the noun with which it is connected is either (1) the *nomen rectum* of a "status constructus," or (2) dependent upon a preposition (which may or may not be expressed; cf. *Ninrag*, p. 12 : 13, *šu-mu-šú* = *qa-ti-ia* (for *ina qa-ti-ia*); *l. c.*, p. 42 : 17, *kur-ra-ša(g)* = *šadâ-a* (for *ana*, *ina šadê*), etc.); or (3) a noun in long *ê* (cf. *par-ṣe-ia* = *me-mu*, *B. E.*, XXIX, No. 7 : 44, see below, p. 44) or long *û*, *a-bu-u-a*, "my father(s)." The last two examples may, however, be translated also by "of (by) my commands," "of (by, to, etc.) my fathers."

that the Sumerian texts of the Assyrian king's library are not always faultless. Hence any attempt at writing, at this time, a Sumerian grammar on the basis of the Ashshurbânapal texts only must necessarily be disastrous. The Sumerian grammar must be based *exclusively* upon texts emanating from a time when the Sumerian was still spoken.

The Nippur Temple Library, with its almost appalling number of sign-lists, syllabaries, lists of phrases, lists of grammatical forms, with its many and various classical Sumerian texts, is bound to become the first and foremost source for the reconstruction of the Sumerian lexicon and grammar.

SOME SUMERIAN EPICS FROM THE TEMPLE LIBRARY OF NIPPUR.

III

THE SUMERIAN EPIC ENTITLED *LUGAL-E ŬG ME-LÁM-BI NER-GÁL*, OR "THE ROYAL LORD, THE FEARFULNESS OF WHOSE STORM IS AWE-INSPIRING."

1. The Literature.

It is the great merit of Dr. Friedrich Hrozný to have pointed out[1] that the several inscriptions of the Library of Ashshurbânapal and of the Berlin Museums, belonging to the series *lugal-e ŭg me-lám-bi ner-gál*, are not, as was generally supposed, hymns to NIN-IB, but represent parts of a *great epic*, "*das man passend šîmâti Ninrag, 'Schicksalsbestimmungen Ninrags,' betiteln könnte*," an epic which records how NIN-IB "*Steine anspricht und ihr Schicksal bestimmt.*"

At least 13 tablets of this epic are known. Hrozný, *l. c.*, pp. 22–39, published and translated the following:

(*a*) *From the Library of Ashshurbânapal.*

A[1]. K. 4827; *Ninrag, Tafel* XI and p. 22. On account of the fragmentary condition of this tablet, it is impossible to determine the name of the stone addressed by NIN-IB. This tablet was followed, according to the "catchline," by one beginning with:

[1] *Sumerisch-babylonische Mythen von dem Gotte Ninrag* (*Ninib*) (*Mitteilungen der Vorderasiatischen Gesellschaft*, 1903, 5), pp. 1, 3.

A^2. [*ur-sag É-šu-me-d*]*u-ta*(?) *gir-è*[1]

mé-šú gǐr-im-ma-ab-úl-[*úl*]

"The hero coming (or lightening up) out of Eshumedu,

to the battle, lo, he went."

B^1. K. 2863 (=IV. R^2., 23, No. 2) = *Ninrag*, p. 32. The name of the stone is lost. The "catchline" informs us that the next tablet began with

B^2. [*ur-sag KA*]*-dúb*[2]*-ba-šú*

ša(*g*) *šu-bi ši-íb-ri*

"The hero in expostulation (lamentation)

upon (towards) the heart his hand, lo, he laid (brought)."

C^1. K. 4814 = *Ninrag, Tafel* XII and p. 34. Also here the name of the stone is broken off. According to the "catchline" the tablet immediately following this began with

C^2. [*ur-sag* . .]*-ra-dím*[3] *mu-bi*

kur-ra ḫa-ba-dú(*g*)

"The hero, whose name is like [. .]

(in)to the land, behold, he called."

D. K. 2871 + 81-2-4, 396 = *Ninrag, Tafel* XII and pp. 36ff., also published by Macmillan, *B. A.*, V, pp. 676ff. This tablet contained the fates of at least three stones,[4] but their names are not preserved.

[1] Hrozný, *l.c.*, p. 22 : 7, reads [. . .] *É-GIR ud-du*, etc., and renders: "[. . .] *trat aus Egir heraus und ging zur Schlacht.*"

[2] Hrozný, *l.c.*, p. 32, Rev. 5, translates: [*Der Held liess den . . . . Stein*], *um* (*ihn*) *zu zerschmettern, aus seiner Hand herunterfallen.*"

[3] Hrozný, *l.c.*, p. 34 : 15, [. . . *ding*]*ir-ra-dím*, etc., ". . . *wie* [*einen Go*]*tt nenne das Land seinen Namen.*"

[4] (1) Obv. 1–26; (2) Obv. 27—Rev. 25 (or 30); (3) Rev. 26 (or 31)—end.

TABLET XI, published in IV. *R*²., 13, No. 1, cf. also *l. c.*, *Additions*, p. 2, *b*. Translated by Hrozný, *Ninrag*, pp. 22ff. It contains the fate or curse of the following stones:

(*a*) The name of this stone is broken off, but from *A. S. K. T.*, p. 81 : 23 (cf. above, p. 6, note 5), we know that the ${}^{n\acute{a}}$*SAG-KAL* stone has to be supplied here. Cf. p. 22, *δ*.

(*β*) ${}^{n\acute{a}}$*esi* = ^{abnu}*ušû*, "dolerite," Obv., 1–32;

(*γ*) ${}^{n\acute{a}}$*na*[1] = ^{abnu}*li-'i-i*, or simply *abnu*, Obv., 33–48;

(*δ*) ${}^{n\acute{a}}$*a-lá-lum* = ^{abnu}ditto, Obv. 49—Rev., 14;

(*ε*) ${}^{n\acute{a}}$*ka-gi-na* = ^{abnu}ditto, Rev., 15—end.

(*b*) *From the Berlin Museums.*

The "catchline" of IV. *R*²., 13, No. 1, informs us that the next or *TABLET* XII begins with

ur-sag ${}^{n\acute{a}}$*giš-šir-gal-e*	*ba-gub*
"The hero to the *giš-šir-gal* stone	drew near."

Fortunately, there has come down to us a Neo-Babylonian copy of this tablet, now preserved in the Berlin Museums, bearing the registration mark *V. A. Th.* 251. It is published in Abel-Winckler, *Keilschrifttexte*, p. 60; Hommel, *Sumerische Lesestücke*, p. 122; is translated by Hrozný, *Ninrag*, pp. 28ff., and records the fate or curse of the following stones:

(*α*) ${}^{n\acute{a}}$*giš-šir-gal* = ^{abnu}ditto, "alabaster," Obv. 1–17;

(*β*) ${}^{n\acute{a}}$*KAK-KAB* = *al-ga-mi-šu*, Obv., 18–29;

(*γ*) ${}^{n\acute{a}}$*dŭ-ši-a* = ^{abnu}ditto, Obv. 30—Rev., 4(?);[2]

(*δ*) ${}^{n\acute{a}}$*gir-KA-gal* = *ṣur-ru*, "chalcedony," Rev. 5–24.

[1] IV. *R*²., No. 1 : 33, 34 ought to be read:

lugal-mu [${}^{n\acute{a}}$*n*]*a*(!)	*i*[*m-ma-gub*]
be-lum [*a-na*] *ab-ni*	*i*[*z-ziz-ma*].

Notice that in *A. S. K. T.*, p. 81 : 23, the ${}^{n\acute{a}}$*UZ* (or *ŠE-ḪU*(*RI*)?) takes the place of the ${}^{n\acute{a}}$*na* and ${}^{n\acute{a}}$*a-lá-lum* here.

[2] As the lower part of this tablet is broken away, it is doubtful whether the beginning of the Reverse belongs to this or another stone.

TABLET XIII begins, according to the "catchline" of *V. A. Th.* 251, with

ur-sag ^{na}*im-ma-na* *ba-gub*
"The hero to the *im-ma-na* stone drew near."

(*c*) *From the Temple Library of Nippur.*

Thanks to the rich treasures of the *Nippur Temple Library,* the number of tablets belonging to this epic can now be increased by three, viz., *B. E.*, XXIX, Nos. 7 and 6 + 8, and the names of stones mentioned on them by the following:

(*α*) ^{na}*gug* or *sâmtu*, "porphyry," *B. E.*, XXIX, No. 6, Rev., II, 1–4;

(*β*) ^{na}*ŠU-U* and ^{na}*GA-SUR-RA*, *l. c.*, ll. 5–17;

(*γ*) *B. E.*, XXIX, No. 6, Obv., and No. 8, Rev. IV, where, however, the names are, unfortunately, not preserved.

(*δ*) ^{na}*SAG-KAL*, *B. E.*, XXIX, No. 7 : 1–13=No. 6, Rev. II, 18–20 + No. 8, col. II, 1–4. Cf. p. 21, *a*, and p. 6, note 5, *a*.

The tablet published in *B. E.*, XXIX, No. 7, is especially noteworthy and important, being a duplicate of IV. *R*[2]., 13, No. 1. It helps us to restore tablet XI (see above, p. 21) in its entirety, at the same time enabling us to give, at last, a coherent and intelligent translation of its most difficult text.

The reasons why these tablets, though apparently without any colophons,[1] do belong to this epic have been given above, p. 13, 11.

[1] In this connection it ought to be noticed that by far the greater number of the texts from the Nippur Temple Library are *without* colophons are subscriptions. Their absence, therefore, is by no means an indication that such tablets are not a part of the Library. It would be an interesting question to examine into the time when or the circumstances under which these colophons were introduced. I am sure that such investigations would yield most important results. Of course there are preserved, in the Nippur Temple Library, quite a number of tablets with this "literary earmark" (written either at the end or on the (upper) left edge of a tablet), but their ratio to the others without a subscription is about 1–10.

2. The Scope and Purpose of the Epic.

Hrozný, who was the first to translate the available inscriptions of this confessedly most difficult[1] epic, thinks (*Ninrag*, p. 3) that its chief purpose (*Haupidee*) consisted in this: "*Es will die Allmacht der Sonne und vor allem den Einfluss der letzteren auf die Natur verherrlichen.*"

I must confess that I fail to see in this epic the slightest indication that NIN-IB was ever considered to be the "sun."[2] On the contrary, wherever one looks, whatever passage one reads, NIN-IB is, and always appears as, the god of the powers of nature, who fights the battles for his faithful against their common enemies. When addressing some of the stones, he "cries," "thunders," "roars"—surely such are not the characteristics of the sun. The fate (*nam-tar*) or curse (*aš-sar*) of the several stones is always given in proportion or with reference to their past or possible future usefulness in the several battles which NIN-IB has fought or intends to fight for his people. The more useful or faithful or less obstinate a stone has been in these battles the better is its fate.

The chief idea expressed in this epic is rather that NIN-IB is the *mušîm šîmâti* or "determiner of fates." Now it is a well-known fact that this title is ascribed in the Babylonian religion only to those gods who played, at one time or another, the *rôle* of the "Son," *i.e.*, of the "Son" who as god of the powers of nature was in a position to fight and overcome the enemies of his "Father" and of his people, hence we are told again and again that "NIN-IB,

[1] Says A. Jeremias, quoted by Hrozný, *Ninrag*, p. 2: "*Besondere Schwierigkeiten bieten dem Uebersetzer die 'Ninib-Hymnen'* IV. *R.*, 13 *und K.* 133. *Solange wir nicht den liturgischen Bau dieser 'Hymnen' verstehen, müssen wir auf das Verständniss verzichten.*"

[2] Cf. for the present my discussion of *Nin-Girsu* = *NIN-IB*, in *Creation Story*, pp. 40ff.; *Bêl, the Christ*, p. 44; *B. E.*, XVII[1], pp. 21, 39; *Hilprecht Anniversary Volume*, pp. 421ff., and see my forthcoming *Hymns and Prayers to NIN-IB.*

the *son of Enlil,*" determined the fate of the several stones. Marduk, *e.g.*, the "Son" of the Eridu trinity, after having overcome the old enemy, the dragon, Tehôm or Tiâmat, the darkness, receives as his reward the *Anu-Enlil*-ship and together with it the *dup šimâti, i.e.*, "the tablets of fates," "the power and right to determine the fates."[1] The position of Marduk, the "Son," being merely an imitation of the *rôle* of NIN-IB, the "Son," it follows that NIN-IB likewise must have overcome the "old enemy" or "primeval waters." A hymn which celebrates NIN-IB as the "saviour" of Babylonia from its enemies—both historical and mythical—will be published in *B. E.*, XXIX, Nos. 2 and 3. After describing the sorrowful and miserable condition into which the land of Babylonia had been thrust:

"When ravaging enemies as if with darkness
the land with destruction had filled,
"When the gods of the land
into captivity they had led,
"When the 'pick and the shovel'
they had made us to carry,
"When but taxes
they had made to be our reward[2] (wages);"

and how, on account of this misery, the Babylonians cry out to NIN-IB for help, this hymn informs us[3] that:

"The lord, who his gracious ears,
behold, inclines,
"NIN-IB, the son of Enlil,
graciously listened:

[1] See *Bêl, the Christ*, pp. 48, 54, and *passim*.
[2] *B. E.*, XXIX, No. 2 : 2–5.
[3] *Ibidem*, ll. 13–20.

"Heaps of stones in the mountain
he heaped up.
"He, who like a passing cloud
by his own strength moves about,
"Who like a fastness over his people
keeps guard:
"A complete change (destruction)
has brought about;
"The hero—he has cast down,
the cities as one he has destroyed,
"The 'mighty waters'
with stones he has conquered."

After the "enemy *(a-ri)*" or "mighty waters *(a kala(g)-ga)*" have been overcome by the "stones" made by NIN-IB in the "mountain," perfect order is restored, the fields produce corn and grass in abundance and

"In granaries like 'tells'
the heaps he has heaped up."[1]
By doing all this,
"The designs of the 'gods'
grandly he has carried out,"[2]

and receives in consequence of this the adoration and the worship of the people:

"Him, yea, NIN-IB and his Father
forever one must reverence."[3]

But more than this, he marries now the goddess *Nin-maḫ*

[1] *L. c.*, l. 30.
[2] *Ibidem*, l. 32.
[3] *L. c.*, l. 33.

or *Bêlit-ilî,* "the mistress of the gods (= Ishtar)," is made like *Anu* and receives the crown of Enlil:

"The hero, he is like *Anu,*
against his wrath none is who can prevail;
"Lord he is! with Enlil's crown (*men*)
his head, lo, is adorned!"[1]

The succession of events described in the above-given hymn is the following:

1. The misery of the land and its people, brought about by the enemy.
2. The delivery and victory by NIN-IB, the "Son and Saviour."
3. The restoration of peace, order and abundance.
4. The carrying out of the designs of the gods, *i.e.,* "the determining of the fates."
5. The marriage or reuniting with "Mother" earth.
6. The exaltation and receiving the highest name, viz., the name of "God (*An* = *ilu*) the Lord (*Enlil*)."

This is found in connection with every "Son" (*Enlil, Nin-Girsu, Sin, Shamash, NIN-IB, Marduk, Nabû*) of a given Babylonian trinity.

Now as the "determining of the fates" follows upon, and is the reward of, a preceding victory over the enemy, it becomes at once evident that the "stones" addressed in this epic which are, apparently, personified and pictured as being arraigned before NIN-IB, must be the *representatives* of the various mountains or countries where they "live"[2] or are found. Thus by determining *their* fates or curses, NIN-IB *ipso facto* determines the fates or curses of the countries or people represented by these

[1] *L. c.,* ll. 39, 41.

[2] No. 7 : 61, *ti(l)-la* = *bal-ṭu.*

stones. To illustrate this by one[1] example, I may be permitted to quote from the fate of the dolerite. Its fate is apparently a reward for past valor and faithfulness:

"Dolerite, thou, who in my battle(s)
forever hast been a hero,
"Thou, who like (dense) smoke ascending
the enemies, lo, hast enveloped,
"Thou, who against me thy arm hast not raised,
thy head hast not thrown back,[2]
'Thou, who during rebellions
'the "Lord," he alone (a) hero is!' lo, hast proclaimed,
"'NIN-IB, son of Enlil, who is like unto thee!'
because, lo, thou hast said,[3] therefore, etc."

Actions and deeds like these are not those of stones but of living persons:—of the people represented by the dolerite. Magan or the "upper mountains"[4] has always—even during rebellions—been faithful to NIN-IB and to the "land of Babylon (*kalam*);" therefore,

"If a king for the prolongation of his life
his name, lo, inscribes,
"If his statue for future days,
lo, he builds,"

he shall make use of Magan's representative stone and bring it into the Nippurian(!) *É-ninnû,* erecting it there as an ornament for all time to come. By doing this the king will acknowledge on the one hand his gratefulness to the dolerite, *i.e.*, to Magan,

[1] Cf. here also note 6 to No. 7 : 54, below, p. 53.

[2] *I.e.*, hast not behaved haughtily towards me.

[3] *B. E.*, XXIX, 7 : 17–21, see below, p. 36.

[4] Magan has to be sought in the *north* of Babylonia, *i.e.*, possibly in Elam or Armenia, not in Arabia.

on the other he will set an example unto the generations to come, showing them how valor and faithfulness are always rewarded.

This explanation of the epic's scope and purpose furnishes us also a key to the possible date of its composition.

Originally Babylonia consisted of "the low- and the highland," *i.e.*, of Shumer and Akkad, *Ki-en-gi-ki-BUR-BUR*; at some still unknown time the faithful of Enlil, under the leadership of NIN-IB, were able to expand their boundaries farther north over the mountains of Elam, Armenia and the Westland, which now likewise came to be known by the name *BUR-BUR*, "highland."[1] Our epic, therefore, must have been composed soon after the *subjugation* of, and victory over, all those mountains which yielded the several stones here mentioned, *i.e.*, when (Enlil and) NIN-IB had advanced from the position of *en kalam-ma*, "lord of Babylonia," to that of *en kur-kur-ra*, "lord of the world."[2] Hence, though there are no stones in Babylonia, though every stone there found and recovered by the various expeditions was imported from distant lands, NIN-IB can determine their fates, because the mountains yielding them had become, in consequence of his victory over them, a part of Babylonia.

Whether these fates or curses are, in one way or another, connected with the "sentiments" attached to the "stones of the twelve months" or "birthday stones" is, at the present at least, difficult to say and this for several reasons:

(*a*) We neither know the exact number[3] of stones mentioned in this epic, nor are we acquainted with their names.

[1] See also *B. E.*, XVII[1], p. 47, note 5.

[2] Cf. also *B. E.*, XXIX, "NIN-IB's position in the Sumerian period of the Babylonian history and religion."

[3] As there exist at least 13 tablets of this epic and as each tablet contains, in all probability, the names of 5 stones (cf. p. 21, Tablets XI, XII), it becomes clear that some 65 stones must have been mentioned. Possibly this epic consisted, originally, of 14 tablets with 5 stones each or 70 stones in all.

(*b*) Even if their names were known to us, we would still have to identify them with our modern equivalents. Hence as long as this is impossible just so long no definite answer to this question can be given.

IV.

TRANSLATIONS.

IN order to gain a more definite idea of the contents and literary arrangement of this epic, I beg to submit in the following pages some "sample fates," selecting for this purpose five stones:

(1) The *ŠU-U* and $^{n\acute{a}}$*GA-SUR-RA* stone, known to us from the Nippur Temple Library only, hence without a Semitic translation.

(2–4) Three stones, duplicates of which (with a Semitic translation) are to be found in the Library of Ashshurbânapal.

(5) One, of which a Neo-Babylonian duplicate (with a Semitic translation) is preserved in the Berlin Museums.

The *literary scheme* of this epic is quite artificial and poetic consisting most generally of the following parts or subdivisions:

(*a*) The approach of NIN-IB.

(*b*) His addressing the stone while sitting down, or crying to it, or mustering it, etc.

(*c*) His determining the fate, giving

(*α*) the reason for the fate, and

(*β*) the fate itself.

(*d*) An "editorial annotation,"[1] which, however, is wanting in some, if not most, cases.

The *language* of this epic is a curious mixture of *EME-KU* and *EME-SAL* forms.[2]

[1] See above, p. 11, *ε*.

[2] Cf. *me-ir-ri* = *gĭr*, *B. E.*, XXIX, No. 6, Rev. II, 10; the infix *en-ṣí-en* for *en-ṣi-en*, *l.c.*, l. 12; *zu-ba* for *zub*, No. 7 : 15; 8 : 5; *ge* = *gi* = *me-en* = *gin*, *mèn*, 7 : 40, note; *si-gi* = *sí*(*g*), 7 : 54; and others, for which see the notes.

The *writing* or *script* is that of the Old Babylonian period as practiced during the II. dynasty of Ur, c. 2700–2400 B.C.

1. The ^{ná}*ŠU-U* and ^{ná}*GA-SUR-RA* Stone.

Above, p. 6, note 5 *b*, I have indicated that the ^{ná}*ŠU-U* was the last stone of the 10th tablet of our epic and that in all probability it is the same as the ^{ná}*SU-U* = ^{abnu}ditto of *A. S. K. T.*, p. 81 : 23, 24, which latter is written also ^{ná}*SU-Ú*. If their identity be maintained, we would have to read ^{ná}*šu*(*su*)-*u*(*ú*). Its modern equivalent is still unknown. The reading ^{ná}*GA-SUR-RA*, though the most probable one, is nevertheless doubtful. In l. 9 the *ga* has *three* double wedges at the end. Are these to be connected with the first wedge of *SUR*, reading ^{ná}*Ú-in*(?)-*gar-ra* = "the stone which produces strength," and taking the whole as an explanatory apposition to ^{ná}*šu-u*? Against this explanation speaks, however, the suffix *en-ṣi-en*, l. 11. Otherwise there is nothing known about this stone.

The fate of these stones may be transcribed and translated as follows:

B. E., XXIX, No. 6, Rev., II, 5–17.

(Cf. Photographic Reproductions, pl. I, No. 2.)

5. [*ur-s*]*ag-e* ^{ná}*ŠU-U* ^{ná}*GA-SUR-ra-ge*
   gù-ám-ba-de

   The hero to the *SHU-U* and the *GA-SUR-ra*,
   to them, behold, he spoke,

6. *en-e a-ri-a-dé*
   ib-šid[1]*-dé*

   The lord, while sitting down
   and mustering them,

7. ^{d}*NIN-IB dumu* ^{d}*En-lil-lá-ge*
   nam-ám-mi-íb-tar-ri

   NIN-IB, the son of Enlil,
   their fates, lo, he determines:

8. *náŠU-U gishḫug*[2]*-mà*[3]

sabu-dím za-na-dím

"*SHU-U stone!* (thou who wast) for my weapon

like a winged torch,

9. *náGA-SUR-ra gud-dím*

šà-na-ba-an-láḫ[4]*-gi-en-[ne-dím]*

"*GA-SUR-ra* stone! (thou who wast) like a steer

that never had been led into captivity:

10. *am-dím á saḫar*[5]*-ra*

me-ir-ri-dím za-na-dím

"'Like (unto) a mountain-ox of untold strength,

with winged feet,

11. *BIR*[6]*-dím*

šu-ḫa-ba-e-en-ṣi-en

"'Like (unto) a *BIR*

strength shall be given you!

12. *ní me-lám-mu*

ba-e-en-ṣí[7]*-en-du(l)*

"'My awe-inspiring splendor

shall cover you!'"

13. *á-maḫ-ni*[8] *la-ba-an-zi(g)-gi-en*

z[a-na-dím]

"Their sublime strength shall not be one which can be removed,

or like a fleeting one,

14. *kù-dím-e zi-ni-šú*[9]

ḫe-[en-s]í(g)-[sí(g)-e]

"The worker in gold, on account of their lustre,

shall set them,

15. *simug ki-nam-dumu*[10]*-ni-šú*

[. . . . . .]

"The (gold-) smith at the 'place of their childhood'

[shall look for them]

16. *ú-sag*[11]
dingir-ri-e-ne-ge
"The *U-sag*
of the gods

17. [*me-te*(*n*)-*n*]*a-uš*[12](?*da*?) *usug-gi*[13]
ḫe-im-ne-si-si-sá
"As an ornament in the temple
shall set them up."

NOTES.

1. *I.e.*, by taking into his hands first the one and then the other stone. Or is the sign *šid* rather that of *ra* = *ramû*, *ašâbu*, hence parallel to *a-ri-a*? The construction is here, as elsewhere, this: NIN-IB spoke while determining their fates; *nam-ám-mi-ni-íb-tar-ri* is, therefore, a circumstantial clause, hence standing in the present tense, indicated by the overhanging vowel.

2. See below, p. 47, note 8.

3. *Mà* here better than *gà*.

4. *I.e.*, like an untamed steer.

5. Which has strength as plentiful (*saḫar* = *turpu'u*, *turpu'tu*) as the dust. Cf. Cyl. A, 16 : 20, *guškin saḫar-ba*, "gold like dust," *i.e.*, in such quantities.

6. Signification unknown. Cf., however, *C. T.*, VI, 9, col. I, 19, 43; II, 7, 15, 33; 56–58(?) on all these places a certain kind of stone is distinguished by either *DUB*(= plate) or *PA* (? or *ŠU?GIŠ*? = shaft?) or *BIR* (= block?).

7. The various phonetic values, registered in Br. 9688–9698, belong to the sign *NE* (not to the group *KI-NE*); cf. *NE* = *ni-e* = *kinûnu*, M. 3090 = *KI-NE* = *ni-e* or *gu-un-ni* = *kinûnu*, Br. 9703, hence *NE* = *KI-NE* stand to each other in the same relation as *ág* = *ki-ág* = *râmu*. If this be true, then *NE* is also = *ṣí*, Br. 9698, and *en-ṣí-en* = *en-ṣi-en*, l. 11. However, a reading *ní me-lám* | *mu-ba-e-en* | *gì-en-du*(*l*) = "the awe-inspiring fear (splendor) | which I give (spread) | shall cover you (them)," might likewise be considered.

8. NIN-IB turns away from the stones and addresses the assembly of the gods or the people of the land. Cf. the fate of the *Algamêshu* stone, l. 2, but especially l. 6, *za-e ḫ*[*e-sà*] with the parallel *mu-bi ḫe-en-s*[*à*], see pp. 56, 58.

9. *Šú* = *ana*, giving the "reason why," though rarely used, seems to be preferable to "in his wisdom."

10. *I.e.*, where they are *born, found.*

11. Cf. *SAúG-ga*, Cyl. A, 13 : 14 = *galuKúA-ga* of the parallel passage in Statue B, 3 : 15, both of which Thureau-Dangin translates by "*Zauberer?*" Cf. also *Ú-KA* = *ú-suk-ku*, *H. W. B.*, p. 108*b*. Seeing that *KA* has the value *sù*, this latter must be abbreviated from *sŭ(g)*, of which *sag* is simply a variant, hence *ú-sŭ(g)* = *ú-sag* = *ú-suk-ku* = (*a*) a certain room sacred to a god, (*b*) the god who occupies that room. The *ú-sag* of the gods was in every case the "Son" of the several Babylonian trinities. This is evident from the Tamūz hymns, where the subscription *edin-na ú-sag-gà-ge* cannot be translated with Zimmern, *Tamūz*, p. 219, No. 3 : 1, 2, by *ana ṣi-e-ri, ki 'i-ru-ma*—and this notwithstanding the fact that *sag-gà-gà* (*sic*!) = *âru*—but must be rendered by "to the abode of the *usagga*, to her husband (*dam-a-na*! or *-ni-šú*), when (= overhanging vowel *-te(g)-ga*!) she drew near."

12. The sign looks rather like *da*. Cf. No. 7 : 29; see below, p. 40.

13. Lit., "into the temple shall bring them," with the *i*-vowel expressing direction, cf. *an-ni*, "towards heaven," Cyl. A, 9 : 11, 16; 17 : 18; 19 : 14; 25 : 8, 16; 27 : 8, etc. With *usug* = *usug-An* = *ešrêtu* cf. *É* = *É-An* = *bîtu*, *i.e.*, "temple," *H. A. V.*, p. 410, note 2, end.

2. THE *náesi* = *abnuušû* OR "DOLERITE."

This stone is the second mentioned on the XI. tablet of our

From the Temple Library of Nippur.

B. E., XXIX, No. 7 : 14–29 = No. 8, col. II, 5–14.

(Cf. Photographic Reproductions, pls. III, No. 4, and II, No. 3.)

14. (5) *lugal-mu náesi-a(e)*
im(ba)-ma(caret)-gub
My royal lord to the dolerite,
to it, lo, he drew near,

15. (6) *ša(g) ḫúb[1]-ba-ka gi-ni-eš zu-ba[2]*
sír-ri-eš im-mi-(íb-bi)
In the midst of his dwelling like a flame (?) flashing up,
with voice raised high, to it, behold, he cries,

---

*Translated by Hrozný, *Ninrag*, pp. 23ff., in this wise:

(14) 2. *Der (königliche) Herr [trat] auf den Dolerit [zu],*

epic. For the identification of the ${}^{n\acute{a}}$*esi* with our "dolerite," see Jensen, *K. B.*, III[1], p. 40, note *. On account of its hardness, being composed of augite and labradorite, it was especially adapted for the purposes here mentioned. The first thing the enemy did or tried to do, when encountering a statue, was either to decapitate it or to make it unrecognizable by chopping off its nose, for both statue and man lose their identity by not possessing this their most prominent feature. Hence it was necessary that one of the hardest and most endurable stones should be selected for this purpose. All of the larger statues so far unearthed are of dolerite, which seems to have been imported into Babylonia chiefly from Magan.[1] For the most probable explanation of its fate see above, p. 27.

In order to facilitate a comparison between the texts of the Library of Nippur and those of Ashshurbânapal, I have given both in transcription here, at the same time adding the translation by Hrozný. The several texts and translations read:

From the Library of Ashshurbânapal.

IV. *R.*,[2] 13, No. 1 : 1–32.

(Hronzý, *Ninrag*, pp. 22ff.)

(14) 1. [*lugal-mu* ${}^{n\acute{a}}$*esi-a*]
[*ba-gub*]
2. *[*be-lum a-na ú-ši-i*]
[*iz-ziz-ma*]
(15) 3. *ḫar-sag gi-dím GUR*(?!)-[*ba*]
[*sír-ri-eš im-mi-íb-bi*]
4. *ina šadî*^i^ *ki-ma* [(see note 2)]
[*ki-ma ṣa-ri-ḫu i-ṣar-ra-aḫ*]

---

(15) 4. *im Gebirge wie Rohr* wankte er . . . ,

[1] Cf. p. 27, note 4.

16. (7) *dNIN-IB dumu dEn-lil-lá-ge*
nam-ám(im)-mi-[ib-tar-r]i
NIN-IB, the son of Enlil,
its fate, lo, he determines:

17. (8) *nâesi mé-ma*
a-ga-ba[3] kúr[4]-ra
"Dolerite! thou who in my battle(s)
forever hast been a hero,

18. (9) *i-izi(-dugud)-dím ma-an-dū*
ù-[mu-un-sí(g)-sí(g)-ga]
"Thou who like (dense) smoke ascending
the enemies, lo, hast enveloped

19. (10) *á nu-mu-e-zi(g)-gà[5]-a-ra*
sag-nu-mu-e-[íl[6]-la]
"Thou who against me thy arm hast not raised,
thy head hast not thrown back,

20. (11) *lul[7]-ám en áš-ni ur-sag*
[gù-im-mi-de-a]
"Thou who during rebellions 'the "Lord," he alone (a) hero is!'
lo, hast proclaimed,

21. (12) *dNIN-IB dumu dEn-lil-lá-ra(ge) a-ba mu-da-ab-sá*
im-mi-dú(g)-[ga]
"'NIN-IB, son of Enlil, who is like unto thee!'
because, lo, thou hast said:

---

(16) 6. *Ninrag, der Herr, Sohn Bêls, [bestimmt] sein [Schicksal]:*
(17) 8. *„Dolerit, der du in meiner Schlacht . . . !*
(18) 10. *wie schwerer Rauch . . . [du] . . . ,*

(16) 5. ^{d}*NIN-IB en dumu* ^{d}*En-[lil-lá-ge]*
[nam-mi-ni-íb-tar]-ri
6. ^{d}ditto *be-lum mar* ^{d}ditto
[šim-tam i-ša-an]-šù

(17) 7. ^{ná}*esi mé-mu*
a-[ga-ba kúr]-ra-ab
8. *ú-šu-ú ša ina ta-ḫa-zi-ia*
[ana aḫ-ra-a-ti (or *edišši̇ka?*) *zi(na?)-ka]-ru*

(18) 9. *i-izi-dugud-dím [ma-an-dū]*
[ù-mu-un-sí(g)-s]í(g)
10. *ki-ma qut-ri kab-ti [te-te-la-a]*
[ta-al-ma-a nak]-ri

(19) 11. *á-zu nu-mu-un-íl-la-[a-ra]*
[sag-nu-mu-e-zi]-a
12. *id-ka la taš-ša-a [(ana ia-a-ši?)]*
[la taš-qa-a re]-ša

(20) 13. *lul-la-ta en-e áš-ni [ur-sag]*
[gù-im-mi-de-a]
14. *ina sar-ra-a-ti be-lum e-diš-ši-šu [qar-ra-du]*
[tab-ba-a]

(21) 15. ^{d}*NIN-IB en dumu* ^{d}*En-lil-lá-ge a-ba [mu(!)-da-ạb-sá]*
[im-mi-dú(g)-ga]
16. ^{d}ditto *be-lum mar* ^{d}ditto *man-nu i-ša-an-na-an-[ka]*
[taq-ba-a]

---

(19) 12. *deinen Arm erhobst du nicht . . . ,*

(20) 14. *in den Feindseligkeiten den Herrn allein* [liessest] *. . !*

(21) 16. *‚Ninrag, Herr, Sohn Bêls, wer ist [dir] gleich . . . ?*

22\. (13) (*kur igi-nim*[8]*-ta*)
ḫe-mu-e-zi(*g*)-[*gi-eš*]
"Therefore, from the 'upper mountain'
they shall remove thee,

23\. (14) (*kur Má-gán-ta*)
ḫe-mu-e-[*ĕ-eš*]
"From the mountain of Magan
they shall lift (fetch) thee!

24\. *z*[*a-e urudu ni*(*g*)]-*kala*(*g*)-*ga*
su-dím ù-[*mu-un-bír-bír-ri*]
"Thou who the mighty bronze (weapons)
like a skin, lo, hast torn to pieces,

25\. *e*[*n me-en á*] *nam-ur-sag-gà-mu*
šu-gal-bi dú-[*dú-a-mu*]
"I, the lord, (thee), the arm of my hero-ship,
greatly I will adorn:

26\. *luga*[*l ti*(*l*)-*la ŭg-su*(*d*)]-*da*
mu-[*ni íb-gà-gà*]
"'If a king for the prolongation of his life
his name, lo, inscribes,

27\. *alan*-[*bi ŭg-ul*]-*lī-a-áš*
[*ù-me-ni-íb-dím-ma*]
"'If his statue for future days,
lo, he builds,

---

(22) 18. *Aus dem oberen Lande möge* ent[fliehen] . . . ,
(23) 20. *von dem Berge Makkans möge man* entfernen . . . ,
(24) 22. *Du* [durchbrennst] *das mächtige Kupfer wie Haut!'*
(25) 24. *Ich bin Herr! Für meinen heldenhalften Arm* [*bist du*] *herrlich* ausgeschmückt.

(22) 17. *kur igi-nim-ta*
ḫe-mu-e-[zi(g)-gi-eš]
18. *iš-tu šadî e-li-ti*
li-in-na-[si-ḫu-ka]

(23) 19. *kur Má-gán-na-ta*
ḫe-mu-e-[ĕ-eš]
20. *iš-tu ša-ad Ma-ag-gan*
lul-lu-u-[ka]

(24) 21. *za-e urudu ni(g)-kala(g)-ga*
su-dím [ù-mu-un-bír-bír-ri]
22. *at-ta e-ra-a dan-nu*
ki-ma maš-ki t[u-šar-ri-ṭu]

(25) 23. *en me-en á nam-ur-sag-gà-mu*
šu-gal-bi dú-[dú-a-mu]
24. *be-lì-ku a-na i-di qar-ra-du-ti-ia*
ra-biš [u-šak-li(a)l-ka]

(26) 25. *lugal ti(l)-la ŭg-su(d)-da*
mu-ni íb-gà-[gà]
26. *šar-ru ša ana ba-laṭ ûmê^{me} ru-qu-ti*
šum-šù i-šak-ka-[nu]

(27) 27. *alan-bi ŭg-ul-lī-a-šú*
ù-me-ni-íb-dím-[ma]
28. *ṣa-lam-šu a-na ûmê^{me} ṣa-a-ti*
i-ban-nu-[u]

---

(26) 26. *Der König, der seinen Namen zum Leben ferner Tage set[zt],*

(27) 28. *seine Statue für die Tage der Ewigkeit anfertigt,*

28. *É-[ninnû*[9]*] ŭ-[di(?)]*
[é KA-zal si-a]
"'Into the *É-ninnû*, (the place) of wonders,
the temple full of delights,

29. *[ki-a-nag*[10]*]-gà i[m-ši-túm*[11]*]*
[me-te(n)-a-šú ḫe-[mu-e-si-si-sá]][12]
"'To the place where one (*i.e.*, the gods) drink(s) water,
lo, he shall bring thee,
for an ornament he shall erect thee.'"

---

(28) 30. *in Éninnû, dem Hause, das vo[ll] von Freude [ist],*

Notes.

1. For pronunciation see *B. E.*, XXIX, No. 2 : 35, note 37. The habitation of NIN-IB, according to IV. R^2., is the *ḫar-sag* or "mountain," but in II. *R.*, 50 : 5 *a*, we are told that the *É-im-ḫar-sag*, *i.e.*, "the house of the 'storm' of the mountain," is one of the names of the *ziggurrats* of Nippur (*En-lil*[ki]), hence "The mountain, the abode of NIN-IB, where he flashes up like a flame and from which he speaks by means of thunder and lightning," is none other but the *ḫar-sag-kur-kur-ra*, "the mountain of the world" (cf. also *Bêl, the Christ*, p. 22), the habitation of Enlil himself. Thence the "Son" is sent out to do his "Father's" bidding.

2. NIN-IB, like the Jahveh of the Old Testament, in the theophanies, reveals himself in and speaks through fire and lightning. *Zu-ba* is in all probability a variant of *zub* = *šupû*, Br. 1217; cf. also *su-ub* = *mašâšu*, Br. 203. The *gur-gu[r]* of IV. R^2. may possibly have been misread for either *su(!)-ba* or *zu-ba*. By translating as given above I consider *gi*, originally *gin*, to be a variant of *NE*, *i.e.*, *gì*, *EME-SAL dé* = *la'bu*, cf. for this interchange *gin* = *gi(n)* = *gì* = *ardatu*, *amatu*, *H. A. V.*, p. 397, note 1, *c*. Of other translations which likewise *may* be possible I mention the following: (*a*) "like a taskmaster (*gi-ni-eš* = *kima mu'irri*) verily (*zu* = *kêniš*, *H. A. V.*, p. 419, note 9) thundering (*gù . . . ba* = *rigmu epêšu*);" (*b*) "truly (*gi-ni eš* = *kêniš*) blessing it (*KA . . . zu-ba* = *KA . . . su-ub* = *karâbu*);" (*c*) "like a *GI* (taskmaster, counsellor, *mâlik*) verily (*zu*) speaking, crying (*KA-ba* = *epêš pî*, *pît pî*, etc.)."

3. Or *a-ga-zu* = *ediššika*, "thou alone"?

4. *Kúr* = [ ]-*ru*(IV. R^2.) may be emended either to [*na-k(a)*]-*ru* or [*zi-ka*]-

(28) 29. *É-ninnû*

é KA-zal [si-a]

30. *ina É*-ditto

bîti ša ta-šil-ta ma-[lu-u]

(29) 31. *ki-a-nag-šú(!) mu-[š]i-túm*

me-te(n)-a-šú ḫe-[mu-e-gà]

32. *a-šar [ša mê lu-bil-ka]-ma*

a-na si-ma-a-ti l[i-iš-kun-ka]

(29) 32. *am Orte des Wassertrinkens . . . zu den Schätzen [leg]e [dich]!"*

ru. If the former emendation be preferred then cf. *B. E.*, XXIX, No. 4, Rev. 15, 16, where it is said of the "lord NIN-IB": *^{galu}kúr-ra é-a-na ^{galu}ḫúl-gál ga-na-nam | úru-na ^{galu}erim ga-na-nam*, *i.e.*, "unto the house of the (NIN-IB's) enemy an adversary, verily, thou (NIN-IB) art | unto his (the enemy's) city a foe indeed thou art." In this case the meaning would be: "Dolerite, thou who in my battle(s) | forever hast been an enemy (*sc.* unto my enemies), hast always considered my enemies to be thy enemies."

5. Seeing that we expect a relative clause (cf.*-íl-la* of IV. *R*².), a reading *mú-a-ra* seems to be out of question. The *ra* at the end signifies the *dative*.

6. *I.e.*, thou hast not behaved proudly, haughtily towards me, but didst as commanded by me. For *sag-íl* = *sag-zi* = *šaqû ša rêši* in this signification see also Jensen, *K. B.*, VI¹, p. 402.

7. *Lul* = *sarrâti* = lit. "Treulosigkeiten," Jensen, *l. c.*, pp. 324, 354.

8. *I.e.*, the mountains at the *north* of Babylonia, of which *Má-gán* was in all probability a part. Others seek Magan in (southern) Arabia.

9. The *É-ninnû* is *here* apparently another name for the temple *É-kur* of Nippur inhabited by the "Father" Enlil and his "Son" NIN-IB, hence the same as the *ḫar-sag*, the *ḫúb-ba* of Enlil and NIN-IB, l. 2. Notice also that *ninnû* (50) is the *number* of Enlil *and* NIN-IB (Br. 10,036f.) and that it has the gloss *illil*, *i.e.*, *^{d}Enlil*, Br., *l. c.*, and *C. T.*, XXIV, 5 : 40; hence it would, perhaps, be better to read here *É-illil*. That this very same name should signify also the temple of *^{d}Im-gig^{ḫu}-bar-bar*, *i.e.*, *^{d}Nin-Girsu* = *^{d}NIN-IB*, of Girsu, is by no means strange; it is, in fact, a corroboration of my statement in *H. A. V.*, p. 413, note 3, and elsewhere, "that the temples of other cities bore the same or similar names as that of Nippur."

10. For the *ki-a-nag* of *É-ninnû* at Girsu cf., among other passages, also Cyl. A, 22 : 15, *ki-a-nag dingir-ri-ka a im-nag-nag-a*, "*An dem Wasserort der Götter, wo sie (die Götter) Wasser trinken.*" For other references see Thureau-Dangin, *S. A. K. I.*, p. 72, note *c*.

11. See above, p. 10, *δ*.

12. See above, p. 33 : 17.

3. The *nâe-li-el* Stone.

Noteworthy is the later corruption of the Ashshurbânapal text: *nâa-lá-lum* = *abnu* ditto. In *C. T.*, VI, 11, A, col. I, 48, the *nâZA.ṬU(i.e., ḫulâlu) a-la-lum* (followed by *nâZA.ṬU ú-la-lum*)

From the Temple Library of Nippur.

B. E., XXIX, No. 7 : 38–46.

(Cf. Photographic Reproductions, pl. IV, No. 5.)

38. *lugal-mu nâe-li-el-e*
i[m-ma-gub]
My royal lord to the *e-li-el* stone,
to it, behold, he drew near,

39. *dNIN-IB dumu dEn-lil-lá-ge*
nam-á[m-mi-ib-tar-ri[1]]
NIN-IB, the son of Enlil,
its fate, lo, he determines:

40 *nâe-li-e[l-e] giš-túg-pi-tug kur[2] galuna(d[3])-g[e[4]]*
[ní-mu ḫu-mu-ni-íb-ri]
"*E-li-el* stone! wise one, of the mountain the overpowerer, thou,
my awe-inspiring fear, with it thou shalt be clothed;

---

* Translated by Hrozný, *Ninrag*, p. 27, as follows:

(38) 50. *Der königliche Herr trat auf den Alallu-Stein zu,*

(39) 51. *Ninrag, der Herr, Sohn Bêls, bestimmt sein Schicksal:*

is mentioned, while in V. *R.*, 30, 65 *e, f* (see Delitzsch, *H. W. B.*, p. 73 *b*) we have the writing $^{n\acute{a}}$*ZA.ṬU e-lá-lum.* Is the writing *a-la-lum* to be connected, in one way or another, with the $^{d\ a\text{-}la\text{-}la}$*alan* of *C. T.*, XXV, 23 *c*, 5 (cf. also *Bêl, the Christ*, pp. 17 : 12, 19 : 18, 10) so that the latter would mean "an (unknown) god whose (name was lost but whose) statue was made out of *a-la-lu* stone (instead of dolerite)?" The modern equivalent for *e-li-el* is not yet known. Rev. l. 11 of the Ashshurbânapal text is spurious, it being omitted in the Nippur text.

The text reads:

From the Library of Ashshurbânapal.

IV. *R*^{2}., 13, No. 1, Obv., 49—Rev., 14.

(Cf. Hrozný, *Ninrag*, p. 26.)

(38) 49. *lugal-mu* $^{n\acute{a}}$*a-lá-lum*
ba-gub
50.* *be-lum ana* ^{abnu}ditto
iz-ziz-ma

(39) 51. ^{d}*NIN-IB en dumu* ^{d}*En-lil-lá-ge*
nam-me-ni-íb-tar-ri
[^{d}ditto *be-lu mar* ^{d}ditto]
[*šim-tam i-ša-an-šu*]

(40) 52. [$^{n\acute{a}}$*a-lá-lum giš*]-*túg-pi-tug tug*(! = *kur*!) ^{galu} *ne me-en*
ní-mu ḫu-mu-ni-íb-ri
53. [^{abnu} ditto *ša mâti ra*]*b uz-ni mu-uṣ-ṣa-lu at-ta*
pu-luḫ-tam(*ta*) *lu-u ta*(*tar*)-*ra-ma*

---

(40) 53. „[Wenn] *du den Verständigen befeinden wirst, werde mit Furcht* (*von mir*) *befallen!*

41. *ki-bal-a kalam u[r-ur]-ri-a-mà*[5]
mu-mu ḫ[e-mu-ni-íb-sà-a]
"In hostile land and countries strange to me
my name thou shalt proclaim;

42. *silim-ma-zu-[ta]*
nam-ba-[da-ab-e]
"In thy welfare,
in it a loss thou shalt not suffer;

43. *gûr-ra-zu tur-tu[r-la-b]i*[6]
ḫe-gí(g)-[e or *gi?]*
"An abrogation of thy greatness
shall be impossible;

44. *me-mu bar*[7]*-[z]u*
si-ḫ[a-ra]-ni-ib-sá-e
"My commands by thee,
yea, by thee they shall be executed;

45. *gishḫug*[8] *sī(g)-[sī(g)-ga] ur-sag dig*[9]*-ga-[zu]*
šu-gal-bi ḫe-ni-dú
"In the conflict of weapons, warrior, thou who killest,
gloriously thou shalt be adorned:

} Wanting!

46. *ùg-e ŭ*[10]*[du(g)-]gi-eš ḫe-a-m[ā]*
[ár-e]š ḫe-mi-i-i[11]
"The people shall gladly look upon (turn to thee)
and greatly reverence thee."

---

(41) 2. *Im Feindeslande, (und) gleicherweise im Lande verkünde meinen Namen!*

(42) 4. *In deiner Unversehrtheit werde nicht verkürzt,*

(43) 6. *deine Grösse sei dem Kleinwerden ein Hindernis!*

(41) R. 1. *ki-bal-a kalam ur-a-si-ga*
mu-mu ḫu-mu-ni-íb-sà-a
2. *ina mât nu-kur-ti ina ma-a-ti mit-ḫa-riš*
šu-mi lu-u tam-bi
(42) 3. *silim-zu-ta*
nam-ba-da-ab-e
4. *ina šul-me-ka*
e ta-an(tan)-na-šir(šír)
(43) 5. *gûr-ra-zu tur-tur-la-bi*
ḫe-gí(g)
6. *rab-bu-ut-ka el ṣu-uḫ-ḫu-ri*
lim-ra-aṣ
(44) 7. *me-mu bar-zu*
si-ḫa-ra-ab-si-sá-e
8. *par-ṣe-ia ina zu-um-ri-ka*
liš-te-ši-ru
(45) 9. ^{gish}*ḫug sī(g)-sī(g)-ga ur-sag dig-ga-zu*
šu-gal-bi dú-ma-ab
10. *ina tam-ḫu-uṣ kak-ke qar-ra-du ša ta-na-ru*
ra-biš šuk-li-la
11. *kisal-maḫ-e ki-gal-la*
ḫu-mu-un-da-ri
12. *ina ki-sal-ma-ḫi ki-gal-la*
lu-u ra-ma-(a-)ta
(46) 13. *kalam-ma du(g)-gi-eš ḫe-i-i*
ár-ri-eš ḫe-im-me-gál
14. *ma-a-ta ṭa-biš lib-ri-ka-ma*
ana ta-na-da-a-te liš-kun-ka

---

(44) 8. *Meine Gebote mögen gut thun deinem Körper!*
(45) 10. *In dem Zusammenstosse der Waffen, o Held, der du tötest, stirb herrlich,*
12. *in dem grossen Hofe der Unterwelt werde hingelegt!*
(46) 14. *Das Land möge dich freundlich ansehen und verherrlichen!"*

Notes.

1. A circumstantial clause: "he drew near determining the fate."

2. The second *tug* of IV. *R*². has been misread by Ashshurbânapal's scribe or copyist; it ought to be a *kur*.

3. For the same interchange of *na*(*d*) and *ne* cf. (*lì*-)*lí-šú na*(*d*)(*ne*)-*da*, *C.T.*, XV, 27 : 12–15 = 30 : 15–17, and *Hilprecht Anniversary Volume*, p. 400, note 4, end; cf. also *na* = *na*(*d*) = *ṣalâlu*, No. 7 : 59, note 12, p. 54. From this it follows that *mu-uṣ-ṣa-lu* cannot be derived from צלה, but that it has to be taken as a I² or II² of צלל = *muṣṣal*(*l*)*ilu* = *muṣṣallu* = *muṣṣalu*. For *ṣalâlu* in the signification "to spread, lay, stretch, smite down; to overpower, to conquer, to kill," cf. (*KU* =) *ḫug* = *ṣalâlu*, with the variant *ḫub* (*Hilprecht Anniversary Volume*, p. 400, l. 21) = *kamâru*, *ḫatû*, etc.; see also the *galu*ḫ*ùb-bu*, Br. 2690; M. 1764. The *d*Ú*r-ra*(!) *sĭ*(*g*)(!)-*ge*(!) (thus is to be read, not *d*Ú*r ŠUR*[lil], surely an ideograph with a Semitic phonetic complement in the *Sumerian* column is out of question) = *lu-maš*(!) *ṣal-lu-ti*, V. *R*., 28 : 41 *c. d*, is, therefore, not the "*beschattender Gott*" (Delitzsch, *H. W. B.*, p. 568 *a*), but the god *Nergal* (as "Son" of the Kutha trinity, see *Hilprecht Anniversary Volume*, pp. 226 and 227, notes 1, 2), "who stretches, smites down," by means of the lightning or pest, etc., hence *ṣalâlu* is a synonym of *PA*, *i.e.*, *sĭ*(*g*) = *maḫâṣu*, *maqâtu*, *nadû*, etc. This throws also a most welcome light upon the hitherto completely misunderstood passage of Judges 7 : 13, where we read: "Behold, I dreamed a dream, and, lo, a *cake of barley bread*—לֶחֶם שְׂעֹרִים (Qeri צְלִיל) צְלוּל—tumbled into the camp of Midian, and came unto the tent, and smote it (ויכהו) that it fell and turned it upside down, that the tent lay along. And his fellow answered and said, This is nothing else save the sword (חרב) of Gideon." (*a*) It is well known that צלל in Hebrew means neither "to bake" nor "to make a cake." (*b*) It is the great merit of Houtsma to have pointed out, *Zeitschrift für alttestamentliche Wissenschaft*, 1902, pp. 329ff., that the Hebrew לחם, לחום, מלחמה, must denote, in certain passages of the Old Testament, "a weapon" of Jahveh-Elohim. In fact the "cake of barley-bread" is here expressly called a "sword." (*c*) The consonants שׂערים may be read, without any change whatever, שְׂעָרִים from שַׂעַר, "storm" (Jes. 28 : 2); cf. also שְׂעָרָה, "stormwind" (Job 9 : 17; Nah. 1 : 3) and "the stormy wind (רוח סערות)" of Ezekiel, 13 : 11, 13; 38 : 22, see below, p. 55.

The question now arises: "What or who is the cake of barley bread, the sword of Gideon?" One of the most common names of Nergal is *dU-gur*, but *u-gur* is also a *namṣaru* or "sword." Another word for *namṣaru* is *gir-gal*, literally "the great lightning," which latter appears as the weapon (*gish*ḫ*ug*) of *dU-gur* in III. *R*., 69, No. 3 : 80, and of *dNIN-IB* in *Ninrag*, p. 12 *b* : 1, 2, *gú* *gŭr-ru-uš-dŭ-dŭ gir-gal gir nam-An-na-mu mu-e-da-gál-[la-ám]* = *mu-uṣ-ṣir ki-ša-da-a-ti nam-ṣa-ru paṭ-ru ^{d}A-nu-ti-ia na-š[a-ku-šu]*, "the severer of the necks, the sword, the dagger of my *Anu*-ship I carry." For Nergal in the rôle of NIN-IB see *Hilprecht Anniversary Volume*, pp. 426ff. But NIN-IB (*urash*) is = *Laḫmu*, see *Bêl, the Christ*, pp. 17, 18, 19, cf. *l. c.*, pp. 15ff., and *Laḫmu* is the לחם of our passage. From this it follows (*a*) that the לחם or *Laḫmu* is none other than god Nergal, the *ṣâlil* or "smiter," the sword by which the "Father" kills the enemies; (β) that לחם שערים is but a learned gloss to צלול or צליל by an annotator who still knew that the Babylonian Nergal (*ṣâlil*) was identified also with *Laḫmu*, originally, like NIN-IB, the god of the storms: שְׂעָרִים, cf. ^{d}*Nergal* = *ŭg-găl-lu*, "dark storm," *Hilprecht Anniversary Volume*, p. 428, with *l. c.*, p. 422; (γ) צְלוּל לחם שׂערים is not a "*Pumpernickel*," but a line from a "Babylonian list of gods": *ṣâlil* | *Laḫmu ša šârê*; (δ) The passage ought to be read and translated: "Behold, I dreamed a dream, and lo, 'the smiter' (צליל = *ṣâlil*) [gloss: *Laḫmu* of the storms = לֶחֶם שְׂעָרִים = *Laḫmu ša šârê*] rushed into the camp . . . and smote it . . . This is nothing else save the 'sword' (חרב = *namṣaru* = *u-gur*, *gir-gal* = great lightning) of Gideon (who, therefore, must have been a god!)" For לחום, *i.e.*, *laḫû* + mimmation, cf. for the present my remarks in *The Monist*, XVII, No. 1 (January, 1907), pp. 147–149, about *laḫî*, *luḫâ*, occurring in *nom. propr.* like *Mannu-kî-laḫî*, *Mannu-luḫâ*, all of which I would identify with the לחי, "the jaw-bone" of the ass, the weapon of Samson! More about this elsewhere.

4. The traces as given in the copy are absolutely certain. For *ge* the variant of IV. R^2. gives *me-en*; but *me-en* of No. 7 : 58 (p. 52) is represented in IV. R^2. by *gi*, hence *ge* = *gi* = *gin* = *mèn* (*i.e.*, *DU*) = *me-en* (*EME-SAL*) = *atta*, etc.

5. Thus has to be emended on account of the size of the break between *u*[*r*] and *ri*. The *kalam ur-ur-ri-a* are those parts of Babylonia which are still "strange, not subservient to" god NIN-IB. Cf. here the New Testament idea "he who is not with me is against me," hence *ur-ur-ri-a* = "strange, not subservient, inimical."

6. Literally: "(the difficulties in the attempt at) the diminishing of thy greatness shall be insurmountable."

7. For *bar* = *zumru*, with the signification of "power, strength" = *ramânu*, cf. *ní* = *emûqu* = *zumru* = *ramânu* = *á*, see *B. E.*, XXIX, No. 2 : 16, note 14.

8. For this reading cf. above, note 3, and *B. E.*, XXIX, No. 2 : 35, note 37. The ^{gish}*ḫug* or "weapon" is, therefore, a piece of "wood that stretches down" the enemy.

9. For the pronunciation *dig*, *díb* (*EME-SAL*) cf. *Hilprecht Anniversary Volume*, p. 382, note 1, *a*.

10. Emendation doubtful. In view of the Semitic translation *lib-ri-ka-ma*

one might be inclined to read *igi* [*dug*]-*gi-eš* *ḫe-a-mā* (cf. Br. 9311), but the space between *igi* and *gi* is too large; besides, the traces visible after *igi* seem to be those of *é*: *igi* + *é* = *ŭ*. *Ŭ-mā* either = *ŭ-ag*(*-a*) = *bârim*, *R. H.*, 68 : 20 or = *ŭ-mù* = *târu ana*, *ḫîṭu ana*, "to turn to, to look upon," *C. T.*, XV, 13 : 1 = IV. *R*[2]., 28, No. 4, Rev., 5, 6 = *R. H.*, 82 : 9, 10. Cf. also *Hilprecht Anniversary Volume*, p. 393 : 71.

11. Literally: *ina tanadâti li'udka* or *litta'idka*.

4. THE *nâka-gi-na* STONE.

The Semitic name of this stone, though rendered here by *nâ*ditto, was, according to *A. S. K. T.*, p. 81 : 23, 24, *ša-da-nu*,

From the Temple Library of Nippur.

B. E., XXIX, No. 7 : 47–61; ll. 52–59 = No. 6, Rev., III, 1–8.

(Cf. Photographic Reproductions, pls. IV, 5; I, 2.)

47\. *ur-sag-*[*e n*]*âka-gi-na*
ba-gub
The hero to the *ka-gi-na* stone
drew near,

48\. [*nam*]*-kala*(*g*)*-*[*ga-bi-šú*]
gù-ba-an-de-[*e*]
Crying
with all his might;

49\. [*dNIN-IB dumu dEn-lil*]*-lá-ge*
nam-ám-mi-i[*b-t*]*ar-ri*
NIN-IB, the son of Enlil,
its fate, lo, he determines:

50\. [*šul ní-tug*]
giš-šir bar[1]*-šú gál-kam*
"Hero, awe-inspiring one,
whose lustre spreads to all sides,

* Translated by Hrozný, *Ninrag*, pp. 27ff., as follows:

(47) 16. *Der* (*königliche*) *Herr trat auf den „Bergstein" zu,*
(48) 18. *aus seiner Kraft schreiend,*

which Hrozný, *Ninrag*, p. 67, renders by "*Bergstein.*" But is not practically every stone a "mountain-stone?" In *C. T.*, VI, 11, *a*, col. I, 1–5, are mentioned the $^{n\acute{a}}$*ka-gi-na*, $^{n\acute{a}}$*ka-gi-na ti*(*l*)-*la* (cf. No. 7 : 61, below, p. 52), $^{n\acute{a}}$*ka-gi-na làḫ-ga*(= shining, brilliant), $^{n\acute{a}}$*dub* (= plate) *ka-gi-na*, $^{n\acute{a}}$*ŠU*(?*PA*?*GIS*? = shaft?) *ka-gi-na*. According to No. 7 : 50, it was a stone of lustre (*giš-šir*, cf. *làḫ-ga* above), precious and valued like refined gold (*l. c.*, l. 58), being found in the *Naïri* lands, Tigl., VIII, 12. Cf. also Zimmern, *B. B. R.*, p. 138 : 2.

The text may be transcribed and translated as follows:

From the Library of Ashshurbânapal.
IV. R^2., 13, No. 1, Rev., 15–43.
(Cf. Hrozný, *Ninrag*, pp. 26ff.)

(47) 15. *lugal-mu* $^{n\acute{a}}$*ka-gi-na*
ba-gub
16.* *be-lum ana* ^{abnu} ditto
iz-ziz-ma
(48) 17. *nam-kala*(*g*)-*ga-bi-šú*
gù-[*ba-an-*]*de-e*
18. *ana dan-nu-ti-šù*
i-šes-si
(49) 19. ^{d}*NIN-IB en dumu* ^{d}*En-lil-lá-ge*
nam-mi-ni-íb-tar-ri
[^{d}ditto *be-lu mar* ^{d}ditto]
[*šim-tam i-ša-an-šu*]
(50) 20. *šul ní-tug*
giš-šir igi-bar-ra-šú ni-gál-la
21. *ed-lu na-'i-du*
ša ni-iš nu-ur i-ni-šù ana a-ḫa-a-a-ti šak-nu

---

(49) 19. *Ninrag, der Herr, Sohn Bêls, bestimmt sein Schicksal:*
(50) 21. *„Erhabener Held, dessen Blick seitwärts gerichtet ist,*

51. [^{na}*ka-gi-n*]*a ki-bal-a-ta*
gù-mu-e-ri[2] *gál-la*
"*Ka-gi-na* stone! who in hostile lands
a 'crying for help' hast brought about,

52. [*ga-na*[3] *š*]*u-mu*
sá-nu-mu-ri-ib-dú(g)
"Verily, him who my hand
not has seized

53. [*da-da-a-ta*]
ba-ab-lá[4]*-en*[5]*(a)*
"Among the evil-doers
thou shalt reckon,

54. [*ùg*[6]*-zu gĭr-zu*]
ba-ab-si-gi[7]*-en*[5]
"Under thy people's feet
thou shalt cast!

55. [*me* ^{d}*Babbar*]
me-zu [*ḫ*]*e-a*
"The commands of *Shamash*
be thy commands,

56. [*di-kud-dím kur-kur-ra*]
si-sá-e(caret)
"Like unto the judge of the lands
(thou shalt) execute them!

57. [*gal-an-zu pá-rú*[8]]
[*ni(g)*]*-nam-ma-ka*
"The wise and the knowing one,
whatever his (their) name(s),

---

(51) 23. „*Bergstein,*" *der du im feindlichen Lande furchtbares Getöse hervorbrachtest*

(52) 25. (*den*) *meine Hand nicht siegreich erfasste,*

(53) 27. (*den*) *ich mit den Bösen nicht zusammenwarf:*

(51) 22. $^{n\acute{a}}$*ka-gi-na ki-bal-a-šú*
gù-mir-ra ni-gál-la
23. ^{abnu}ditto *ša ina mât nu-kur-tim*
rig-ma ez-za taš-ḳu-[nu?]
(52) 24. *ga-na šu-mu*
sá-nu-mu-ri-íb-[dú(g)]
25. *šal-ṭiš qa-ti*
la ik-šu-du-šu
(53) 26. *da-da-a-ta*
nam-ba-da-ab-lá-e
27. *it-ti aš-ṭu-te*
la at-ta-da-[aš-šu]
(54) 28. *ùg-zu gìr-zu*
ba-ab-sí(g)-sí(g)-[gi-en]
29. *a-na še-ip ni-ši-ka*
e ta-at-tas-ḫu
(55) 30. *garza* ^{d}*Babbar*
garza ḫe-a
31. *pa-ra-aṣ* ^{d}*Šamaš*
lu-u par-ṣu-ka
(56) 32. *di-kud-dím kur-kur-ra*
si-sá-e
33. *ki-ma da-a-a-ni ma-ta-a-te*
šu-te-šir
(57) 34. *gal-an-zu pá-rú*
ni(g)-nam-ma-ge
35. *[ir]-šù mu-du-u*
mim-ma šum-šù

---

(54) 29. *zu den Füssen deines Volkes werde nicht hingeschüttet!*
(55) 31. *Das Gebot des Šamaš sei dein Gebot,*
(56) 33. *wie ein Richter leite die Länder!*
(57) 35. *Der Weise (und) derjenige, der Jegliches kennt,*

58. [*kù-ŭg*[9] *guškin-šú*]

[*ḫ*]*e*-[*en-n*]*a-kal-li me*(caret)-*en*[10]

"Like gold refined

shall value thee.

59. [*šul ba-dib-ba*[11] *na*-(*ù*-)*ba*]-*ra*(*bar*)-*e*-*ù*(caret)-*un*[12](caret)

en-na[13] *ti*(*l*)-*la-zu-šú*

"Hero, whom I possess(ed), not will I cast thee down,

not as long as thou livest!"

60. [*ì-ne-šú nam-tar-r*]*a* ^d^*NIN-IB-kam*[14]

Now(this) was among the fates (determined) by NIN-IB

61. [*ŭg-da*[15] *kalam-ma* ^ná^*ka-gi-na t*]*i*(*l*)-*la ŭr ḫe-en-na-na*[*m-ma*]

at the time when the *ka-gi-na* stone was found (lived) in the country. (And) thus, lo, it was!

---

(58) 37. *mögen dich gleich Gold wertschätzen,*

(59) 39. *o Held, den ich erfasste, indem ich mich nicht eher (zum Schlaf) legte, bis ich dich zum Leben brachte!"*

Notes.

1. The text of IV. *R*²., which reads *igi-bar*, translates *bar* twice: (a) by *niš*, (b) by *ana aḫâti*. *Igi* as well as *nîš îni* are superfluous here. For a similar redundance cf. *si-sá*, No. 7 : 44, where IV. *R*². has *si-si-sá*, see above, pp. 45, 33 : 17.

2. The *gù-mu-e-ri*, lit. "a crying for help," cf. *gù-ri-a* = ditto (*i.e.*, *na-ra-ru-ut*) *rig-me*, Br. 2566, has become in IV. *R*². a *gù-mir-ra* = *rig-ma ez-za*, "a furious uproar (crying)." Or is *mu-e-ri* simply a graphic (*EME-SAL*) variant of *me-ri*, *mi-rí*, *me-ir*, *mi-ir*, *mir*, *gĭr*, etc. = *ezzu*?

3. *Ga-na* = *šalṭiš* is here an interjection: "Well then!" "*wohlan!*" "verily!" Cf. Cyl. A, 1 : 24; 3 : 22, 23, *ga-na ga-na-ab-dú*(*g*), "*wohlan, ich will sprechen!*"; *R. H.*, 75 : 18, *ga-na ì-dŭ é ma-al* = *a-tu-u bîta pi-tu-u*, "*wohlan, Wächter, öffne*(*t*) *das Haus!*" *Ga-na*, if followed by a verbal prefix beginning with *m*, becomes *ga-nam* with various Semitic equivalents—but all in the above-given signification—see M. 4357ff. F. 3269ff.

4. The expression *da-da-a-ta . . . lá* = *itti aštûte nadû* has here the meaning "to look upon, to consider as, to reckon among, the evil-doer(s), wicked person(s)," "*Jemanden* (*als*) *unter den Feinden* (*seiend*) *wissen und ihn danach*

(58) 36. [*kù-ŭg*] *guškin-šú*
ḫe-en-kal-la-gi
37. *ki-ma ḫu-ra-ṣi*
li-ša-ki-ru-ka
(59) 38. *šul ba-dib-ba na-ù-ba-ra-e-ne*
ti(*l*)*-la-zu-šú*
39. *ed-lu ša ak-mu-ka-ma a-di ú-bal-li-ṭu-ka*
la aṣ-la-lu-ma
(60) 40. *i-ne-šú nam-tar-ra* ^{d}*NIN-IB-ka-ta*
41. *i-na-an-na ina ši-ma-a-ti ša* ^{d}ditto
(61) 42. *ŭg-da kalam-ma* ^{ná}*ka-gi-na ti*(*l*)*-la sìr-sìr ŭr ḫe-na-nam-me*
43. *ûmê*^{me} *ina ma-a-ti* ^{abnu}ditto *bal-ṭu iq-qab-bi ši-i lu-u*
ki-a-am

---

(60) 41. *Heutzutage wird gesagt: ,Als Ninrag die Schicksale festsetzte,*
(61) 43. *(waren) Stürme im Lande, (war) der ,,Bergstein'' lebendig.' Die (Gestirn)-vorzeichen also!*

behandeln." For *lá* = *nadû* in this signification cf. *lá* = *amâru* and Jensen, *K. B.*, VI[1], p. 486, *nadû* = "*hinwerfen, zeichnen, im Kopfe entwerfen?*" The axiom is: "He who is not with me is against me"; "my enemies are and must be thy enemies!"

5. Seeing that *en*(*a*) indicates a relative clause, the literal translation of ll. 52ff. would be: "Verily, (with regard to) him who my hand not has seized (to seize the hands of somebody = to submit to him, to reverence him, to acknowledge him as the master), thou shalt (be he who shall) cast him with (*i.e.*, among) evil-doers, (who shall) trample him under thy people's feet." The spurious *nam* of IV. *R*[2]. made it necessary that l. 53 should be considered to be parallel to the *nu* of l. 52: "Verily, ... him whom with (among) evil-doers I have not yet cast."

6. The stone's people are the inhabitants of the mountains where the *ka-gi-na* stone is found who "have seized the hands of NIN-IB or Enlil."

7. *Gìr-si-gi* = *gìr-sí*(*g*)*-sí*(*g*) = *ana šêpâ asâḫu*, "to cast under the feet, to tread, trample upon," is here a syn. of *gìr-sì*(*g*) $^{sa-ag}$*-gán* = *raḫâṣu ša* [*šêpâ*], M. 4969. For the interchange of the various *sig* cf. *sag-si-si-gi* = *sag-sì*(*g*) =

sag-sí(g), "to smite (with a hatchet) upon the head," and see also *sí(g)*, *sī(g)* = *nadû*. For the sign *gan* (*gán*) at the end of words cf. *a-ša(g)* = *a-ša(g)-gan*. The *e* of the Semitic translation is the interjection "*wohlan!*" It cannot be = "not," because the prefix *ba-ab* is never used in a negative sense. A reading *ta-at-taš-pak* is for the following reasons out of place here: (*a*) we expect a *relative* form, parallel to (*t*)*attadâ* and required by the Sumerian *en(a)*; (*b*) a IV^2 of *šapâku* is senseless; (*c*) *ta-at-tas-ḫu* (= *ta'tas(a)ḫu*) fulfills all grammatical requirements; (*d*) from *asâḫu* (syn. of *nadû*, *raḫâṣu*) we have the well-known *tâsuḫtu* = "*Niedergeworfenheit, Zerstörung*," "trampling (under the feet)."

8. Variant of *pá-rí-in*. For reading and signification see *B. E.*, XXIX, No. 4, Rev., 3, note 3.

9. Though it seems that something is missing before *guškin* (see IV. R^2., additions, p. 2), yet the Semitic translation does not indicate it. Is *kù-ŭg* = (*ṣarpu*) *ṣurrupu*, "refined," to be supplied?

10. For *me-en* = *mèn*, *gin(DU)* = *gi* = *ge* = *atta*, see above, No. 7 : 40, note 4, p. 47. Noteworthy is the variant *en* for *me-en* = *gi*.

11. *Dib-ba* = *kamû*, here in the sense of *aḫâzu*, "to take, possess, have": "thee whom I possessed = thee whom I hold, have," see also *Hilprecht Anniversary Volume*, p. 432, note 1.

12. The root of this verbal form is, of course, not *ù*, but *na* = phonetic writing for *na(d)*, *ne*, see above No. 7 : 40, note 3, p. 46. *Ba-ra* = *la*, *e* = present tense, *ù* = either exclamative (*Hilprecht Anniversary Volume*, p. 419, note 5) or emphatic (*l. c.*, p. 401, note 11), *un* = relative, and the whole an emphatic form, therefore *na* put at the beginning: (*ša*) *la aṣ-la-lu-ma*, "as regards the stretching, casting down, lo, I am not (shall not be) he who does it (will do it)," *i.e.*, "verily, I shall *never* cast thee down."

13. For *en-na* (omitted in IV. R^2.!) *ti(l)-la-zu-šú* cf. *en-na . . til-la-áš* = *a-di aš-bu*, II. *R.*, 15 : 9 *a*, hence = "as long as (while) thou 'livest'", *i.e.*, "existest, art in existence (cf. l. 61, *ti(l)-la* = *bal-ṭu*)." The Semitic translation has: "as long as I (am he) who has called thee into being (am in existence)."

14. *Kam* = *ka-ta*: "(this) is (*m*) among (*ra*, *ra . . . ta*) the fates of NIN-IB (*ka*)," *i.e.*, which NIN-IB has determined.

15. *Ŭg-da*, when followed by a verbal form with *-a* or *-ba* or overhanging vowel or both, means "on the day when," cf. *Hilprecht Anniversary Volume*, p. 386, *d*, and note 1.

5. THE $^{n\acute{a}}$*KAK-KAB* = *algamêshu*, "THUNDER-STONE."

The Neo-Babylonian sign for *algamêshu* is written (l. 18) or (l. 28), which Hommel, *Sumerische Lesestücke*,

p. 123, identifies with the Assyrian , Br. 8110ff. This identification can hardly be correct, seeing that the old Babylonian has , clearly an ideogram consisting of *KAK* + *KAB*. The same or a similar Old Babylonian sign is found also in *C. T.*, VI, 11, *a*, col. I, 10–12, where, like here, it is mentioned after the *nágiš-šir-gal* and appears in plates (?*dub*) and shafts (?*PA*). Hommel, *l. c.*, was also the first to identify the Assyrian *algamêshu* with the Biblical אלגביש, which he considers to be the "crystal." What his reasons for this identification are, I do not know. He, like most scholars, probably sees in אלגביש the Arabic article אל (*al*) and גביש (= *gamêsh*) = "ice, crystal (Job 28 : 18)," comparing it with the Ethiopic אבן ברד = "hail-stone, crystal," and the Greek κρύσταλλος = "ice, crystal." If this explanation were correct, we would have here the first trace of the Arabic nation, language and country. But as tempting as this explanation, no doubt, is, our "fate" speaks against it; nor can I imagine that the signification of אלגביש = *algamêshu* is "hail" or "hail-stones"; against this is evidently the determinative *ná* and the fact that "hail-stones" can not be very well "offered unto the gods."

In Ezekiel 13 : 11, 13, we are told that Jahveh smites (the "wall" of) his enemies by means of an "overflowing shower (גשם שוטף)," "*algamêshu* stones (אבני אלגביש)" and a "stormy wind (רוח סערות, cf. above, p. 47, the לחם שערים)," to which are added, *l. c.*, 38 : 22, "the fire (אש)" and "the brimstones (גפרית)." These three or five weapons are clearly those of "the god of thunder, lightning, storm, rain and clouds." We miss, however, the lightning or thunderbolts, if the אבני אלגביש be the "hail-stones." Considering this difficulty, I am inclined to see in the *algamêshu* the "thunderbolts, thunderstones," "weapons (*giš*) which cut off the life (*kin-ti*)" of the enemy, or which "subdue (*kab* = *kamâru*) everything (*KAK*=*dū*)," having to read, therefore, [nd]*dū-kab*. It may not be impossible that *algamêshu* has to be analyzed as consisting of *algam* + *êš* or *îš*; *algam* may be an *'af'al* form of *lagâmu* = *ragâmu* (cf. *Lagam-ar* = לעמר, Gen. 14 : 1, and [d]*Šâgimu* = *Rammân*), "to thunder," and *êš* or *îš*, a foreign (Elamitic?) word for "stone," cf. the יש in חלמיש, "pebble" (and the ית in גפרית, "brimstone)." If this explanation were true, it would agree exactly with the suggestion made above (p. 28) that the several mountains yielding these

From the Temple Library of Nippur.

B. E., XXIX, No. 8, col. III, 1–6.

(Cf. Photographic Reproductions, pl. II, 3.)

1. *lugal-mu* [[nd]]*KAK-KAB* [*im-ma-gub*]
   igi-dul[1]-[*im-ma-an-ag*]
   My royal lord to the *Algamêshu* stone, to it, lo, he drew near,
   an angry look upon it, lo, he cast;
2. *en íb-ba kalam-ma*
   gù-mu-na-[*de-e*]
   The lord in anger (in)to the land,
   (in)to it he cries,
3. [d]*NIN-IB dumu* [d]*En-lil-lá-ge*
   aš-im-ṁi-ib-sa[*r*[2]*-ri*]
   NIN-IB, the son of Enlil,
   a curse against it, lo, he utters:
4. *a-dím gin-mu-šú*
   LI-mu-e-[*ši-tar*]
   "As (seeing that) against 'my going'
   thou hast counseled me

---

* Translated by Hrozný, *Ninrag*, p. 31, as follows:

(1) 19. *Der Held trat auf den Algamîšu-Stein zu, sah ihn* (*zornig*) *an*,

(2) 21. *der Herr spricht grimmig im Lande die Rede*,

stones are, in all probability, those of Elam and Armenia (occupied by the Elamites).

This "thunderstone" receives a "curse (*aš-sar*)," *i.e.*, it becomes *tabû*, "sacred to (because cursed by) the gods." Strange to say that the thunderstone has not lost, even at our present time, its "curse," seeing that the most curious superstitions are still connected with it.

The "fate" of the "thunderstone" reads:

From the Berlin Museum.

V. A. Th. 251 (written in Neo-Babylonian characters), Obv., 18–29.

(Cf. Abel-Winckler, *Keilschrifttexte*, p. 60; Hommel, *Sumerische Lesestücke*, p. 123; Hrozný, *Ninrag*, p. 30.)

(1) 18. *ur-sag* [ná]*KAK-KAB ba-gub*
igi-dul-ba-an-ag
19.* *qar-ra-du ana al-ga-mi-ši iz-ziz-ma*
it-te-kil-me-šu
(2) 20. *en-e íb-bi kalam-ma*
gù-mu-un-na-ni-íb-bi
!21. *be-lum ag-giš ina mâti*
a-ma-ta i-qab-bi
(3) 22. [d]*NIN-IB en dumu* [d]*En-lil-lá-ge*
aš-ám-mi-ni-íb-sar-ri
23. [d]ditto *be-lum mar* [d]ditto
ir-ra-ar-šu
(4) 24. *a-dím gin-mu-šú*
LI-mu-e-ši-in-tar
ki-ma a-na a-la-ki-ia
taš-ta-lu

---

(3) 23. *Ninrag, der Herr, Sohn Bêls, verflucht ihn:*
(4) 24. „*Wie du für meinen Zug* (fest)gesetzt *hast,*

5. *giš-kin-ti*[3]*-mà*

igi-ba gin-na

"(therefore) before my *kiškitte,*

before them thou shalt go!

} Wanting!

6. *nd*[4]*KAK-KAB sá-dú(g)*[4] *ŭg-[da] gù[r-ru]*

za-e ḫ[e-sà]

"'*Algamêshu* stone! an offering (unto the gods) whenever gathered'

thou shalt be called!"

---

(5) 25. *unter den Schildträgern gehe vorn einher!*

27. *Um etwas zu thun, erhebe das Haupt!*

NOTES.

1. *Dul* is probably a variant of *gul,* which latter is a synonym of, and parallel to, *ḫul,* R. H., 81 : 6 = IV. *R*²., 28, No. 4 : 13, cf. *gu-la* parallel to *ḫul, C. T.,* XV, 7 : 10. If so, *igi-dul-ag* may best be translated by "frowned upon."

2. The *Algamêshu* stone receives a curse. The reason for this curse is given in l. 4: it had decided or advised *against* the "going" of NIN-IB. What this "going" was is hard to tell. Seeing, however, that *alâku* is also a syn. of *dâku,* and remembering that one of the standing attributes of NIN-IB is = *dâ'ik šadê,* it may be possible that the Algamêshu stone had advised NIN-IB against "the smiting of the mountain," *i.e.,* against the smiting of the *people* of the mountain where the algamêshu stone "lived."

3. What the *kiš-kit-te-e* are, is not yet made out. Muss-Arnolt, p. 450, translates it by "workmen," or a "kind of weapon." Delitzsch, *H. W. B.,* p. 350 *a,* leaves it untranslated, but on p. 564 *a* (*sub* צור) he reads *giš-kin-ti* = *is-qi-ti,* thinking that the latter may be = *isqatu, l. c.,* 147 *b,* "*Fessel, Bande.*" Jensen, *K. B.,* VI¹, p. 456 (cf. p. 575), considers it to be "*Jemand, der mit dem KIT-Holz zu thun hat oder dieses selbst*"; in Leander, *Sumerische Lehnwörter,* p. 11, this very same scholar translates our word by "*Schnitzmesser.*" Hrozný, *Ninrag,* p. 72, renders it by "*Schildträger.*" The *EME-SAL* form is either *mu-uš-ki-*

(5) 25. *giš-kin-ti*

igi-šú al-gin

ina kiš-kit-te-e.

ina ma-aḫ-ri a-lik

26. *ni(g)-dím-dím-ma-zu*

sag-ga ḫa-za-ab

27. *ana mim-ma e-pi-ši-ka*

ri-e-ša ki-il

(6) 28. ^{ná}*KAK-KAB sí-dú(g) ŭg-da ni(g)-gùr-ru*

mu-bi ḫe-en-s[à]

29. *al-ga-me-šu sa-at-tuk ina na-še-e*

šu-ma-[šu in-na-ab-bi]

---

(6) 29. *,Algamîšu, Stiftungsopfer der Stürme in Darbringung' nen[nt] seinen Namen!"*

in-ti or *mu-uš-kin-ti*, which M. 753, following his predecessors, transcribed by *qis-qat-tu-ú*. On account of the absence of *galu* before *giš-kin-ti*, it becomes evident that the *kiš-kit-te-e* cannot be *here*(!) a *class of soldiers*, but must be weapons, more particularly "weapons (*giš* = *mu-uš*) which cut off (*kin*) the life (*ti*)." This explanation is corroborated by a passage in *C. T.*, XXIV, 35 *a*, 19–22, where the following 4 *giš-ki[n-ti* ^{d}*NIN-IB-ge*] are mentioned:

19. ^{d}*Šar-*	*ū[r*	*šu*	]
20. ^{d}*Šar-*	*ga[z*	*šu*	]
21. ^{d}*Al-gàm*(!)*-meš*(!)	[	*šu*	]
22. ^{d}*Ŭg-ba-nu-il-lá*	4 *giš-ki[n-ti* ^{d}*NIN-IB-ge*		]

For ^{d}*Šar-ūr* as a weapon of NIN-IB cf., among other passages, especially *Ninrag*, p. 12 : 19, 20, *á-zi(d)-da-mu* ^{d}*Šar-ūr-mu mu-e-da-gál-la-á[m]*; for ^{d}*Šar-gaz ibidem*, ll. 21, 22, *á-kab-bu-mu* ^{d}*Šar-gaz mu-e-da-gál-la-á[m]* and for ^{d}*Ŭg-ba-nu-íl-lá*, *l. c.*, ll. 25, 26, *mes kur-gul-gul* ^{d}*Ŭg-ba-nu-íl-la-mu mu*(*sc.*, *e-da-gál-la-ám*). In l. 21 the copy of *C. T.*, XXIV, gives ^{d}*Al-*, *i.e.*, *ENGAR*, for which I propose to read ^{d}*Al-*, *i.e.*, *gàm-meš*, identifying it with *al-ga-me*(*i*)*-šu* of our inscription here. While the ^{d}*Šar-ūr* is at the right and ^{d}*Šar-gaz* at the left, the ^{d}*Al-gàm-meš* goes before (*igi-gin*) ^{d}*NIN-IB* and thus *leads* the other weapons. From this it follows that the ^{d}*Ŭg-ba-nu-íl-lá* took, in all probability. its place behind (*egir*) NIN-IB. Cf. here the similar description of ^{d}*Nin-Gir-su* in my *Creation Story*, p. 41.

4. Though the Algamêshu stone is cursed, yet he shall be an "offering" *sc.* unto the gods—clearly the first instance, in the Sumerian inscriptions, of what the Hebrews called a *tabû*: *cursed* and hence *sacred!*

V.

A FRAGMENT OF THE SUMERIAN EPIC *AN-DÍM DÍM-MA*, or, "THOU WHO LIKE ANU ART MADE," FROM THE TEMPLE LIBRARY OF NIPPUR.

Above[1] I have pointed out that, after he had overcome the enemies of Babylonia, *i.e.*, the Guti, Lulubi and Elamites,[2] NIN-IB was made "like Anu" and was crowned with "the crown of Enlil." This exaltation of NIN-IB to equal rank with the "God and Lord" of Babylonia, with Enlil of Nippur, is repeatedly referred to in the Sumerian and later Assyrian literature; cf., *e.g.*, such passages as Hrozný, *Ninrag*, p. 12 : 9, *ní me-lám An-dím dugud-da-mu*, "the fearfulness of my glory is as weighty as that of Anu;" *l. c.*, p. 14 : 7 *u*, *ŭg An-na-dím* [ ], "storm [full of awe-inspiring fear] like Anu;" *l. c.*, p. 16 : 16, [*An-n*]*a*(!) *á-gal-a-ni-šú pa*(*d*)-*da me-en*, "I am he whom ([*ša*]) Anu has chosen (called) in his great might." Thus it happened that NIN-IB, in the several lists of gods, is identified with Anu; cf. *Bêl, the Christ*, pp. 16–19. At the time when the epics and hymns from the Nippur Temple Library were written, Enlil had already displaced Anu and had himself become the "God *par excellence*" of Babylonia, *i.e.*, Anu in our texts here is nothing but an attribute of Enlil. This is the reason why we find passages like *Ninrag*, p. 40 : 19, *An* ^{d}*En-lil-da zag-*

[1] See p. 26.

[2] See Hilprecht, *B. E.*, Ser. D, Vol. V, fasc. 1, p. 23, and my review of this book in *Old Penn*, March 19, 1910, p. 370.

di-a, "he (NIN-IB) who had been raised to equal rank[1] (*ina šit-nu-ni-šu*) with Anu-Enlil[2]," or I. *R.*, 29 : 18, where NIN-IB is called the *ši-na-at*[3] *^{d}A-nim u ^{d}Da-gan*, *i.e.*, "the equal of Anu-Dagan(= Enlil[4])," or why names like *^{d}L*, *^{d}En-kur-kur*, *^{d}SUḪ*, *^{d}Lugal-banda*, etc., signify both Enlil and NIN-IB.

The epic which praises NIN-IB as the equal of Anu-Enlil is apparently the one under discussion here. It began with the two opening lines:

An-dím dím-ma[. . .],
^{d}NIN-IB ^{d}En-lil-dím d[*ím-ma* . . .]
i.e., "thou who like Anu art made [. . .]
NIN-IB, thou who like Enlil [art made' . . .]"

Though we know[5] that this epic consisted originally of six tablets, yet so far two[6] only have been recovered from the Library of Ashshurbânapal, and these are unfortunately in a fragmentary condition. It is, therefore, impossible to state, at this time, anything definite with regard to both its character[7] or its contents.

True it is, that the little fragment of this epic, from the Temple Library of Nippur, published here in photographic

[1] Thus is to be translated, cf *.B. E.*, XXIX, No. 1, col. III, 37, [^{d}]*Kur-gal tu(d)-da* [*dumu*]*-a-ni zag-nu-di*, "(NIN-IB) begotten by the 'Great Mountain,' his son without (*nu*) equal (*zag-di*)."

[2] The Semitic translation has *itti ^{d}A-nim u ^{d}En-lil*. For this *u explicativum* see *The Monist*, October, 1906, p. 635.

[3] Stands for *šin-na-at*, root *šanânu* = *zag-di*; cf. also Delitzsch, *H. W. B.*, p. 676 *b*.

[4] See *C. T.*, XXIV, 6 : 22 = 22 : 120, *^{d}Da-gan* | *šu* (*i.e.*, the same as on the left side) *^{d}En-lil*. This shows that Enlil must have been known, in one city or another, by the name of Dagan. For another similar case cf. *Hilprecht Anniversary Volume*, p. 416 *a*.

[5] See above, p. 13

[6] Whether II. *R.*, 19, Nos. 1, 2 also belong to this epic (as Hrozný thinks) has, in view of the absence of their colophons, to remain doubtful.

[7] *I.e.*, whether it is an *epic* or only a *poem*.

reproduction,[1] does not shed any new light on these questions, yet its existence is most important, and this mainly for the following reasons:

1. It gives us an idea of the character and contents of the Nippur Temple Library.

2. It demonstrates anew that certain literary productions of the Library of Ashshurbânapal must have been in existence as early as 2500 B.C.

3. It exhibits interesting and instructive linguistic[2] and graphic[3] variants.

4. It justifies the hope that not only the rest of this tablet may be recovered in the near future, but that other similar texts will be found in the Temple Library of Nippur.

Our little fragment begins with l. 15 of K. 2864, thus showing that the first seven lines of the Sumerian inscription have been lost. They, or at least the beginning of them, may be restored, however, according to Hrozný, *Ninrag*, p. 6. While the Obverse belongs to the first, the Reverse gives us a part of the sixth tablet. What has been preserved represents a dialogue between NIN-IB and *ᵈNin-kar-nun-na.* The context is about the following: NIN-IB praises his mighty accomplishments and utters kind words to his son (*sic*!) and servant *ᵈNin-kar-nun-na;* thereupon (see *Ninrag*, p. 16 : 7ff.):

The gracious words

of NIN-IB

Nin-karnunna

after having heard them

[1] See pl. V, Nos. 6, 7.

[2] Cf. *ša(g)-ga* = *ša(g)-ga-zu* and *gù-mu-un-na-de* = *mu-un-na-ab-bi*, Rev., l. 5; *lugal-la* = *lugal*, l. 6; *a-nun e-ri-a* = *a-nun-na a-ri-a*, l. 7; *ŭg-ba* (cf. also above, p. 16, notes 1, 4) = *ŭg-bi-a*, l. 8; *ni(g)-nam-ḫe-ám* = *ŭg nam-ḫe-ám*, l. 10; *ni(g)-dú-rú-a-šú* = *ŭg-dú-rú-a-šú*, l. 11.

[3] Cf. *ni(g)-ŠA(G)* + *A* = *ni(g)-ŠAa(G)*, R., l. 9.

And after having drawn near to the lord NIN-IB
uttered this prayer:
"My king, in the city which thou lovest
thy heart may be at rest;
"NIN-IB," etc. Here follows l. 1, of the Reverse.

The rest of this tablet informs us that NIN-IB complied with the wishes of [d]*Nin-kar-nun-na.* The text may be supplied according to *Ninrag,* p. 18 : 15*uff.* The epic ends with an exclamation in praise of NIN-IB:

From the Temple Library of Nippur.

B. E., XXIX, No. 9, Obv.

(Cf. Photographic Reproduction, pl. V, No. 6.)

Beginning broken away.

1. *d*[*umu* [d]*En-lil-la* . . .]
   Son of Enlil . . .
2. *u*[*r-sag ḫuš* . . .]
   Hero, furious one . . . .
3. *dumu* [d]*En-*[*lil-lá* . . .]
   Son of Enlil . . .
4. *me kur-r*[*a* . . .]
   The command of the "mountain" . . . .
5. *me nun-*[*na* . . .]
   The command of the "prince" . . . .
6. *dingir-ri-e-*[*ne* . . .]
   The gods . . . .
7. [d]*A-nun-na*[. . .
   The Anunnaki . . .
8. [d]*NIN-IB á*[1]*-*[*sum-ma*
   NIN-IB, thou (to whom) power [was given . . .
9. *lugal-ra*(?) *gù-*[. . .
   (To) the king [spoke(?).
10. *en* [d]*NIN-IB ur-*[*sag* . . .
   Lord NIN-IB, hero . . .
11. *kur gú erim* [*sí*(*g*)*-sí*(*g*)*-ki*
   Thou (who) all the lands of the enemies [hast cast down . . .
12. *bád ki-bal* [*gul-gul*
   Thou (who) the wall of the hostile land [hast destroyed

Rest broken away.

^{d}NIN-IB dumu-maḫ	*É-kur-ra-ge*
ner-gál a-a muḫ-na	*ZAG-SAL-zu maḫ-ám, i.e.,*
"NIN-IB, sublime son	of Ekur,
"Hero of the father his begetter,	thy exaltedness is great."

If we compare these lines with *B. E.*, XXIX, No. 9, Rev., 5, 6:

[*dumu-sa*]*g ^{d}En-lil-lá*	*^{d}NIN-IB u*[*r-sag*]
[*ner*]*-gál a-a muḫ-na*	*ZAG-SAL-zu m*[*aḫ*(or *gal*)*-ám*]

it may not be impossible that No. 9 formed likewise the last tablet of a larger and similar epic or hymn in praise of NIN-IB.

Our fragment may be transcribed and translated as follows:

From the Library of Ashshurbânapal.

K. 2864

(Hrozný, *Ninrag*, Taf. I, Obv., and p. 6 : 15ff.)

(1)	15.	[*dumu*] *^{d}En-lil-lá*[. . .	
	16.	[*mar*] *^{d}En-lil*[. . .	. . . . *Bêl* . . .
(2)	17.	*ur-sag ḫuš ám*[. . . .	
	18.	*qar-ra-du iz-z*[*u* . . .	*Ein furchtbarer Held* [*bist du*] . .
(3)	19.	*dumu ^{d}En-lil-*[*lá* . . .	
	20.	*mar ^{d}*[*En-lil* . . .	*Son Bêls* . . .
(4)	21.	*me* [*kur-ra* . . .	
	22.	*pa-ra-a*[*ṣ šadî^{i}* . . .	DEIN] *Gebot* . . . .

(5)

Rest broken away.

From the Temple Library of Nippur.

B. E., XXIX, No. 9, Rev.

(Cf. Photographic Reproductions, pl. V, No. 7.)

Beginning broken away.

1. *^{d}N[IN-IB uru ki-ág-gà-zu-šú]*
   [ša(g)-zu ḫe-en-ḫug²-gà]
   NIN-IB, in the city which thou lovest
   thy heart may be at rest;

2. *éš Nibru^{ki} uru ki-á[g-gà-zu-šú]*
   [šag-zu ḫe-en-ḫug-gà]
   "In the house of Nippur, the city which thou lovest,
   thy heart may be at rest!

3. *É-šu-me-du é ki-á[g-gà-zu-šú]*
   [asilal tu(r)-tu(r)-ra-zu-dé]
   "*Eshumedu*, the temple which thou lovest,
   when in rejoicing thou enterest it,

4. *sal-nita-dam-zu-ùr³[ki-el]*
   [^{d}Nin-Nibru^{ki}-ra]
   Unto thy wife, the maiden,
   the mistress of Nippur

5. *ša(g)-ga gù-mu-un-[na-de]*
   [bar-ra gù-mu-un-na-de]
   That which is in (thy) heart tell to her,
   that which is in thy thoughts reveal to her,

---

* Translated by Hrozný, *Ninrag*, p. 19, as follows:

(1) 16. "*Herr, Ninrag, in deiner St[adt], die du lieb hast, möge dein Herz sich beruhigen,*

(2) 2. *in dem Tempel von Nippur, deiner Stadt, die du lieb hast, [möge dein Herz sich beruhigen]!*

From the Library of Ashshurbânapal.

Rm. 117, Obv., l. 15f.; and K. 2829, Rev., l. 1f.

(Hrozný, *Ninrag, Taf.* IX and *Taf.* VIII, also p. 18.)

The latter tablet begins with *B. E.*, XXIX, No. 9, Rev., l. 9.

(1) 15. *en* ^{d}*NIN-IB u[ru-ki]-ág-gà-zu-šú*
ša(g)-zu ḫe-en-ḫug-gà
16.* *be-lum* ^{d}ditto [*ina âli-ka*] *ša ta-ram-mu*
libba^{ba}*-ka li-nu-uḫ*

(2) 1. *éš Nibru*^{ki}*-ge uru-ki-ág-gà-zu*[*-šú*]
[*ša(g)-zu ḫe-en-ḫug-gà*]
2. *ina bît Ni-ip-pú-ri âli-ka ša ta-ra*[*m-mu*]
[*lib-ba-ka li-nu-uḫ*]

(3) 3. *É-šu-me-du ki-dúr ša(g)-du(g)-ga-zu*
asilal tu(r)-tu(r)-ra(!)-z[*u-dé*]
4. *ana É*-ditto *šu-bat ṭu-ub libbi*^{bi}*-ka*
ina ri-ša-a-ti ina e-ri-[*bi-ka*]

(4) 5. *sal-nita-dam-zu ki-el*
^{d}*Nin-Nibru*[^{ki}*-ra(!)*]
6. *ḫi-ir-ti-ka ar-da-ti*
^{d}[ditto]

(5) 7. *ša(g)-ga-zu mu-un-na-ab-bi*
bar-ra-zu mu-un-na-[*ab-bi*]
8. *ša libbi*^{bi}*-ka qi-bi-ši*
ša ka-bít-ti-ka qi-b[*i-ši*]

---

(3) 4. *Wenn d*[*u*] *in Êšumedu, den Sitz deiner Herzensfreude, mit Frohlocken einziehst,*

(4) 6. *sage deine*[*r*] *Gemahlin, der Magd Nin-Nippur,*

(5) 8. *was du auf dem Herzen hast, sage ihr, was du auf dem Gemüte hast,*

6. *enem-du(g) lugal-la*
ŭ[g-su(d)-da-šú gù-mu-un-na-de]
The gracious words of the king
forever communicate to her!"

7. *a-nun e-ri-a*
[d][Nin-kar-nun-na[4]]
He begotten by the "prince,"
Ninkarnunna,

8. *ŭg-ba*
ka[5] SIGIŠŠE-[SIGIŠŠE-ra-ge]
At that time,
at the feast of sacrifices,

9. *ša(g) ni(g)-ŠA(G) +A*
a-[še(d)-dé im-de]
into (out of?) the *kish-ri-e*[6]
poured out fresh(?) water.

10. *ni(g) nam-ḫe-á[m]*
[ne-in-dú(g)-ga-a-ni(na?) . . .]
To him who abundance
establishes,

11. *me ni(g)-dú-r[ú-a-šú]*
[šu-ne-in-dú-a-na[7]]
To him who with the ordinances forever
complies,

---

(6) 10. *sage ihr die freundliche Rede des Königs für ferne (Zeiten)!'*

(7) 12. *Ninkarnunna, die durch die Zeugung des Erhabenen erzeugt ist,* . .

(8) 14. spre[ngte] *dann aus dem Munde des Ausgiessens*

(6) 9. *enem-du(g) lugal*
ŭg-su(d)-da-šú mu-un-na-ab-[bi]
10. *a-ma-ta(tú) ṭa-ab-ta(tú) ša šar-ri*
ana ru-qi-e-ti qi-b[i-ši]

(7) 11. *a-nun-na a-ri-a*
^{d}*Nin-kar-nun-[na]*
12. *ša ri-ḫu-ut ru-bi-e ra-ḫu-u*
^{d}[ditto]

(8) 13. *ŭg-bi-a*
ka SIGIŠŠE-SIGIŠŠE-ra-[ge]
14. *i(e)-nu-šu*
ina pi-i ni-qi-[e]

(9) 15. *ša(g) ni(g)-ŠAa(G)*
a-še(d)-dé i[m(!)-de]
9. *libbi*^{bi} *kiš(z)-ri-e*
me-e [el-lu-ti iš-puk]

(10) 10. *ŭg nam-ḫe-ám*
ne-in-dú(g)-ga-a-ni . . .
[i-nu-ma duḫ-da]
[u-kin-nu-šu]

(11) 11. *me ŭg-dú-rú-a-šú*
PA(?)[= šu-ne-in-dú-a-na(?)]
12. *par-ṣi-šu ana [ûmê]*^{me} *ṣa-a-ti*
a(?)-[= ušaklilu-šu(?)]

---

(9) 9. *dem Inneren der* Vulva, *kaltes Wasser* aus.

(10) 10. *Nachdem er in Fülle geredet hatte,*

(11) 12. *seine Gebote für die Tage der Ewigkeit . . . [bestimmet hatte],*

12. *É-šu-me-[du pa-è-a]*
[. . *dib-ba-da-a-na*]
When to him who to the bright Eshumedu
[. .] goes,

13. [*ša(g)*]*^{d}NIN-[IB-ge]*
[*ba-šá(g)-šá(g)*]
Namely to NIN-IB the heart
had become appeased,

Rest broken away.

---

(12) 13. *zu Êšumedu* emporgeführt *war und* . . . [er]fasst hatte

NOTES.

1. Or any of the following emendations may be made: *á-gál, B. E.*, XXIX, No. 1, col. I, 3; *á-maḫ, l. c.*, col. II, 12, 15; *á-maḫ sum-ma, l. c.*, col. III, 28, 43; IV, 18; *á-zi(d)-da, l. c.*, IV, 13, 14; *á-ḫuš, l. c.*, No. 5, Rev., 3; *á-KAL-maḫ, l. c.*, No. 11, Rev., 4; cf. *C. T.*, XXV, 11 : 24.

2. For the reading *ḫug, ḫúb* = *ku(g), ku(b)* see above, p. 47, note 8.

3. This *ùr* as post-position occurs also in *Hilprecht Anniversary Volume*, p. 438 : 23.

4. In II. *R.*, 59 : 11, 12, *^{d}Gašan-kar-nun-na* | *^{d}Nin-kar-nun-na* | *bar*(!not *dingir*)*-šu-gál ^{d}NIN-IB-ge* is mentioned between the "wife" of NIN-IB and god Nusku. If the writing *gashan* be correct, we would have to see in *^{d}Nin-kar-nun-na* a goddess; as such she is considered by both Hommel, *Sumerische Lesestücke*, p. 47, and Hrozný, *Ninrag*, p. 114. The latter identifies her with the goddess Bau, the wife of NIN-IB. Hommel as well as Hrozný read *^{d}šu-gál*, which the former translates by "*Dienerin*," and the latter by "*Magd*." That *bar-šu-gál* is the correct reading follows from a duplicate of II. *R.*, 59, viz., *C. T.*, XXV, 45 *a*, 6, [*^{d}Nin-k*]*ar-nun-na* | *bar-šu-gál ^{d}NIN-IB-ge*. *Bar-šu-gál* is generally taken in the sense of *gallabu*, "barber." If, therefore, this divinity were a goddess, NIN-IB would have among his servants a *female* barber only. This, however, it seems to me, is altogether too modern. In *C. T.*, XXIV, 7 : 21–26, are mentioned, immediately after the wife of NIN-IB, the following gods:

21. [*^{d}Enim-ma(cf.*49*b*,10)*-ni-zi* | *luḫ ^{d}NIN-IB-ge*
22. ^{d}[ ]*-ni*(?)*-KAL* | *dam-bi dumu-sal ^{d}PA.KU-ge, i.e.*, "his wife, the daughter of Nusku"; a translation "*Gemahl der Tochter des N.*" (*Michatz, Götterlisten*, p. 82) would have to be *dam dumu-sal*.

(12) 13. *É-šu-me-du pa-[è-a]*
[. . d]ib-ba-da-a-na
a-na É-ditto *šu-pú(!)-u*
[iba'u(?)]
(13) 14. *ša(g)* ^{d}*NIN-IB-[ge]*
[ba-šá(g)]-šá(g)
libbi^{bi} ^{d}ditto
iṭ-ṭi-ib

Rest to be supplied according to *Ninrag*, p. 18 : 15 *u* ff.

---

(13) 14. *(da) wurde begütigt das Herz Ninrags.*

23. ^{d}*[Nin-kar-nu]n-na*		*bar-šu-gál* ^{d}*NIN-IB-ge*
24.	[nothing missing!]	*šeš* ^{d}*Enim-ma-ni-zi*
25. ^{d}*Kin[da*(Br. 2707)-?	]	*dam-bi- sal*
26. ^{d}	[ ]	ditto

According to this passage ^{d}*Nin-kar-nun-na* is the *šeš* or "brother" (notice that "sister" is *SAL* + *KU* in these lists, cf. *C. T.*, XXIV, 11 : 40; XXV, 24 *a*, 10) of the *luḫ* or "messenger" of NIN-IB, and the husband of ^{d}*Kin[da-?]*, hence *here* at least undoubtedly a *male* divinity and, if a "barber" at all, a *male* barber. The shaded *gašan* of II. *R.*, 59 : 11, ought, therefore, to be corrected into *umun.* The wife of a god has always the same attributes and functions as her husband. ^{d}*Kin[da-?]* is, therefore, likewise rendered by *gallab(t)u.* But what is the meaning of *gallabu*? Delitzsch, *H. W. B.*, p. 196 *b*, remarked quite rightly "*gallabu, Haarscherer, doch nicht ausschliesslich, vielleicht jeder der mit naglabu hantiert*"; *naglabu* he translates, *l. c.*, by "*Messer oder ein sonstiges Werkzeug zum Schneiden.*" Jensen, *K. B.*, VI^{1}, p. 377, thinks it is "*ein Instrument zum einschneiden, einritzen.*" The literal translation of *bar-šu-gál* is "one who handles the *bar.*" *Šu-gál* is = *šu-i* and the *gír-šu-i* = *naglabu* is "the instrument which *is* handled," hence *gír* = *bar*; for this interchange of *b* and *g* cf. Fossey in *Hilprecht Anniversary Volume*, p. 110, 12. *Gír* is = *paṭru, birqu. Bar-šu-gál* is, therefore, nothing but a syn. of *gír-lal* = *nâš paṭri*, "the sword, dagger or thunderbolt carrier." Cf. here the ^{d}*Nin-sar gír-lal* ^{d}*Nin-Gir-su-ka* (= NIN-IB) or *É-kur-ra-ge, Creation Story*, p. 44, and *C. T.*, XXIV, 10 : 16ff. Notice also that *bar-šu-gál* is = *mubarrimu*, while *burru[mu]* is = *gaz* = *dâku*, "to kill." NIN-IB being the god of the powers of nature, his servant and son (*sic*!), the *bar-šu-gál*, becomes thus one of the *manifestations* of these powers by means of which NIN-IB smites, kills the enemies as with a sword or lightning. *Gallabu* is merely "one who handles a sharp instrument, sword, knife, etc.," not necessarily or exclusively a "barber."

5. Cf. *KA* or *TE-UNU* = *pu-ú-[um]*, *TE-UNU* also = *naptânu* = *KA-gub*, *Hilprecht Anniversary Volume*, p. 442, note 8.

6. The translation of this and the following lines must, on account of their mutilated condition, remain doubtful.

7. For a similar construction cf. *Ninrag*, p. 40: 15ff. and for the *na* at the end of verbal forms, see above, p. 16, note 5.

VI.

PHOTOGRAPHIC REPRODUCTIONS.

TEXT.	PLATE.		C.B.M.	DESCRIPTION.
1, 2	I	Obverse and Reverse of a large fragmentary cuneiform text containing parts of the VIth, VIIth, Xth and XIth tablet of the great Sumerian epic, *lugal-e ŭg me-lám-bi ner-gál*, or "The royal lord, the fearfulness of whose storm is awe-inspiring."	2347	Cf. *B.E.*, XXIX, No. 6.
3	II	Continues the Reverse of Pl. I, No. 2, and contains parts of the Xth, XIth, XIIth and XIIIth tablet of the same epic.	1837 + 1839	Cf. *B.E.*, XXIX, No. 8.
4 5	III IV	Obverse and Reverse of the XIth tablet of the same epic.	11087	Cf. *B.E.*, XXIX, No. 7.
6, 7	V	Obverse and Reverse of parts of the Ist and VIth tablet of the Sumerian epic, *An-dím dím-ma*, or "Thou who like Anu art made."	13301	Cf. *B.E.*, XXIX, No. 9.

1 2

1, 2. OBVERSE AND REVERSE OF B. E., XXIX, No. 6.

1, 2. FRAGMENT OF THE GREAT SUMERIAN EPIC, "THE ROYAL LORD, THE FEARFULNESS OF WHOSE STORM IS AWE-INSPIRING." C. 2500 B.C.

3

3. REVERSE OF B. E., XXIX, No. 8.

3. FRAGMENT OF THE SAME EPIC AS Nos. 1 AND 2. C. 2500 B.C.

4

4. OBVERSE OF B. E., XXIX, NO. 7.

THE XITH TABLET OF THE SAME EPIC AS NOS. 1–3.
C. 2500 B.C.

5

5. REVERSE OF B. E., XXIX, No. 7.

THE XITH TABLET OF THE SAME EPIC AS Nos. 1–4.
C. 2500 B.C.

6

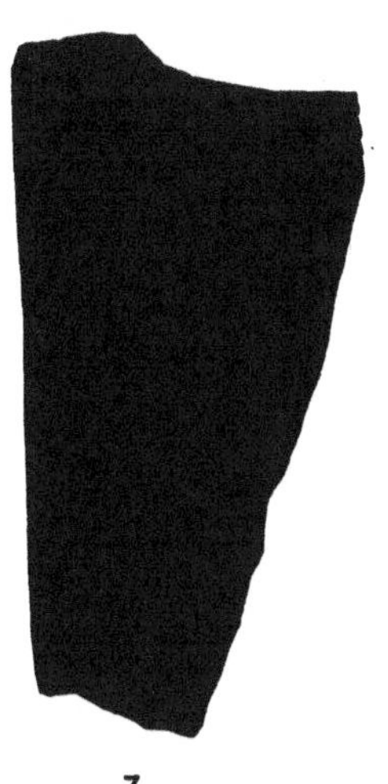

7

6, 7. OBVERSE AND REVERSE OF B. E., XXIX, No. 9.

FRAGMENT OF THE GREAT SUMERIAN EPIC, "THOU WHO LIKE ANU ART MADE."
C. 2500 B.C.

THE BABYLONIAN EXPEDITION

OF

THE UNIVERSITY OF PENNSYLVANIA

EDITED BY

H. V. Hilprecht

The following volumes have been published or are in press:

Series A, Cuneiform Texts:

Vol. I: Old Babylonian Inscriptions, chiefly from Nippur, by H. V. Hilprecht.
Part 1, 1893, $5.00 (out of print).
Part 2, 1896, $5.00.

Vol. III: Sumerian Administrative Documents from the Time of the Second Dynasty of Ur.
Part 1, from the Nippur Collections in Philadelphia, by David W. Myhrman, 1910, $6.00.
Part 2, from the Nippur Collections in Constantinople, by P. Engelbert Huber (ready for press).

Vol. VI: Babylonian Legal and Business Documents from the Time of the First Dynasty of Babylon.
Part 1, chiefly from *Sippar*, by H. Ranke, 1906, $6.00.
Part 2, chiefly from *Nippur*, by Arno Poebel, 1909, $6.00.

Vol. VIII: Legal and Commercial Transactions, dated in the Assyrian, Neo-Babylonian and Persian Periods.
Part 1, chiefly from Nippur, by A. T. Clay, 1908, $6.00.

Vol. IX: Business Documents of Murashû Sons of Nippur, dated in the Reign of Artaxerxes I, by H. V. Hilprecht and A. T. Clay, 1898, $6.00.

Vol. X: Business Documents of Murashû Sons of Nippur, dated in the Reign of Darius II, by A. T. Clay, 1904, $6.00.

Vol. XIV: Documents from the Temple Archives of Nippur, dated in the Reigns of Cassite Rulers, with complete dates, by A. T. Clay, 1906, $6.00.

Vol. XV: Documents from the Temple Archives of Nippur, dated in the Reigns of Cassite Rulers, with incomplete dates, by A. T. Clay, 1906, $6.00.

Vol. XVII: Letters to Cassite Kings from the Temple Archives of Nippur.
Part 1, by Hugo Radau, 1908, $6.00.

Vol. XIX: Model Texts and Exercises from the Temple School of Nippur.
Part 1, by H. V. Hilprecht (in press).

Vol. XX: Mathematical, Metrological and Chronological Texts from the Temple Library of Nippur.

Part 1, by H. V. Hilprecht, 1906, $5.00.

Vol. XXIII: Sumerian Hymns and Prayers to Enlil from the Temple Library of Nippur.

Part 1, by Hugo Radau (in press).

Vol. XXIX: Sumerian Hymns and Prayers to NIN-IB from the Temple Library of Nippur.

Part 1, by Hugo Radau (in press).

Vol. XXX: Sumerian Hymns and Prayers to Tamûz from the Temple Library of Nippur.

Part 1, by Hugo Radau (in press).

Series D, Researches and Treatises:

Vol. I: The Excavations in Assyria and Babylonia (with 120 illustrations and 2 maps), by H. V. Hilprecht, 7th edition, 1904, $2.50.

NOTE: Entirely revised German and French editions are in the course of preparation. The first part of the German edition (*bis zum Auftreten De Sarzecs*) appeared in December, 1904 (J. C. Hinrichs, Leipzig; A. J. Holman & Co., Philadelphia, Pa., sole agents for America). Price *4 Mark* in paper covers, *5 Mark* in cloth.

Vol. III: Early Babylonian Personal Names from the published Tablets of the so-called Hammurabi Dynasty, by H. Ranke, 1905, $2.00.

Vol. IV: A New Boundary Stone of Nebuchadrezzar I from Nippur (with 16 halftone illustrations and 36 drawings), by William J. Hinke, 1907, $3.50.

Vol. V: Fragments of Epical Literature from the Temple Library of Nippur.

Fasciculus 1, The Oldest Version of the Babylonian Deluge Story and the Temple Library of Nippur, by H. V. Hilprecht, $0.75.

NOTE: A German edition is to appear in a few weeks, published by J. C. Hinrichs, Leipzig.

Fasciculus 2, NIN-IB, the Determiner of Fates, according to the great Sumerian epic, "*Lugale ug melambi nergal,*" by Hugo Radau, 1910, $1.00.

(OTHER VOLUMES WILL BE ANNOUNCED LATER.)

———o———

All orders for these books to be addressed to

THE MUSEUM OF ARCHAEOLOGY,

University of Pennsylvania,

PHILADELPHIA, PA.

SOLE AGENT FOR EUROPE:

Rudolf Merkel, Erlangen, Germany.

www.ingramcontent.com/pod-product-compliance
Lightning Source LLC
LaVergne TN
LVHW011120110826
845150LV00008B/2198

* 9 7 8 1 4 2 5 5 7 2 0 0 6 *